▪ HOW SWEET IT IS ▪

■HOW SWEET IT IS■
THE JACKIE GLEASON STORY

James Bacon

St. Martin's Press, New York

HOW SWEET IT IS: THE JACKIE GLEASON STORY. Copyright
© 1985 by James Bacon. All rights reserved. Printed in the
United States of America. No part of this book may be
used or reproduced in any manner whatsoever without
written permission except in the case of brief quotations
embodied in critical articles or reviews. For information,
address St. Martin's Press, 175 Fifth Avenue, New York,
N.Y. 10010.

Design by Laura Hough

Library of Congress Cataloging in Publication Data

Bacon, James, 1914–
    How sweet it is.

    1. Gleason, Jackie, 1916–   . 2. Television
personalities—United States—Biography.
3. Comedians—United States—Biography.   I. Title.
PN1992.4.G6B3 1985   791.45′028′0924 [B] 85-10054
ISBN 0-312-39621-X

10 9 8 7 6 5 4 3

▪ DEDICATION ▪

To my three older children—Carol, Roger and Kathy—
who never missed Reggie Van Gleason the Third, The Poor
Soul, Joe the Bartender, and especially Ralph Kramden on
Saturday nights through the fifties and sixties. I know they
are proud Jackie Gleason chose me to write his biography,
because he is one of their all-time favorites.

■ CONTENTS ■

Sections of photographs follow pages 108 and 172.

■ ACKNOWLEDGMENTS ■

I would like to thank personally everyone mentioned by name in this book, some of them no longer with us, because each one contributed generously in helping me tell the fabulous life story of Jackie Gleason: Audrey Meadows, Art Carney, Frank Sinatra, Toots Shor, Irving Paul ("Swifty") Lazar, Bob Hope, Milton Berle, Jackie Gleason's cousin Renée Wall (widow of the great jockey Nick Wall), Gleason's daughters Geraldine Chutuk and Linda Miller (like her father, a Tony Award actress), Lord Laurence Olivier, Jane Kean, Sheila MacRae, Jan Murray, George Marshall, Elizabeth Taylor, Henny Youngman, Dick Kleiner, Earl Wilson, Jim Bishop, (Kleiner, Wilson and Bishop were all great Broadway columnists in Gleason's heyday on the famous street), Jayne Meadows, George ("Bullets") Durgom, Bobby Hackett (the great trumpet virtuoso in the bands of Glenn Miller and Jackie Gleason), Harry Crane (who wrote the first "Honeymooners" script), Walter Stone and Leonard Stern (who wrote many of the later ones), Jack Donahue, Elvis Presley, Hal Wallis, Maxie Rosenbloom ("Slapsie Maxie," the onetime light-heavyweight champion of the world), Jack Carter, Sammy Lewis, Gene Kelly, Polly Adler (New York's most famous madam), Irving Brecher (creator of "The Life of Riley"), Patsy D'Amore, Gertrude Neisen,

Jack Haley, Flo (Mrs. Jack) Haley, Jack Haley, Jr., Joe E. Lewis, Hal Needham, Honey Merrill, Louis Sobol, Bob Considine, Bobby Darin, Paul Newman, Joel Preston, Burt Reynolds, producer Jennings Lang, Teri Garr, Karl Malden, Dolores Hope, Jack Oakie, Tony Zoppi, Jack L. Warner, Peter Crescenti, Bob Columbe (the latter two are the co-founders of RALPH, the eight-thousand-member-strong Gleason fan club), novelist John O'Hara, Jack Philbin, Billy Martin, Mickey Mantle, Colonel Tom Parker, Bing Crosby, Ed Wynn, June Taylor, Mel Pape, Phil Foster (who started in Brooklyn amateur shows with Jackie) and Buster Keaton—and I hope I didn't forget anybody.

Special thanks go to Marilyn Taylor Gleason, who has been a mellowing influence on The Great One and who has always been charming to me; to Sydell Spear, Jackie's long-time secretary, whose cooperation has proved invaluable in the production of this book; to my wife Doris, who is the most constructive critic I have, sometimes too damn much so. And to Bob Miller, my editor at St. Martin's Press, a very special thank-you. Bob is not only a superb editor, but he is also young (he made me realize, for instance, that hardly any of the younger people out there know that Ed Sullivan was a famous Broadway columnist long before he learned to mispronounce *show* as *shew* on his weekly CBS-TV show).

Finally, I owe it all to Jackie Gleason himself, who first asked me to write this book. He cooperated graciously and honestly, and I was especially touched by some of his descriptions of his early days, which were like something out of Charles Dickens. Jackie—thanks.

▪ FOREWORD ▪

Dear Jim,

I have read the book and it is now time for me to cop out.

An actor is a romanticist, and the mentality of a romanticist is stored in the heart, a dangerous locality for such an important faculty.

His vanity is a worthless gem, tirelessly polished by pride. However, vanity is an actor's courage.

Self-deception thrives in the compost of flattery. He looks into the deceitful mirror of publicity and envisions himself a genius, a hero and a pundit.

There is something noble (and pitiable) about an actor's conceit; it is such a petty weapon with which to wage a war for dignity.

An actor goes through life with failure snapping at his heels like a mongrel, but his ego transforms failure into adversity, and the mongrel into a mere puppy.

I guess there is no way to elude your drinking stories. Many are the times I have ended up wounded by a deep and ugly hangover after a day of wishful drinking.

That, Jim, is the extent of my excuses. However, my philosophy of life is still intact—just play the melody, live, love, and lose gracefully.

—JACKIE GLEASON

▪ PROLOGUE ▪

I consider myself perfectly cast to write the Jackie Gleason story. Who else has ever been officially labeled an "evil companion" for The Great One? Not even Toots Shor, Frank Sinatra, or the great Mickey Mantle, all world-class drinking companions of Jackie's, have enjoyed this privilege.

My somewhat dubious claim to fame came about in Baton Rouge, Louisiana, in 1982, where Jackie was filming *The Toy* with Richard Pryor. I was also there, working with Jackie on this book. Since I am a veteran Hollywood columnist with large circulation, I was given the VIP treatment—chauffeur, limousine, the works.

One morning I called my chauffeur to pick me up at my hotel for a trip out to the set. The driver demurred, suggesting that I call Pete Emmet first. This didn't sound too unusual; Pete was the unit publicist on the picture, and thus privy to all last-minute scheduling changes. I called Pete.

"I don't quite know how to put this to you other than to tell you like it is. It's very embarrassing," said Pete. "You are barred from the set because you are an evil companion for Jackie Gleason."

He was serious, and the news stunned me. In my thirty-seven years in covering Hollywood, I had never before been barred from a set.

"How in the hell," I demanded to know, "can anyone be called an evil companion for Jackie Gleason?"

Pete was sympathetic.

"Hey, I know it sounds crazy," said Pete, an old friend. "But those are my orders. Dick Donner [the director] called Phil Feldman [the producer] in New York and raised hell about you. He said you got Gleason drunk during production. Phil called me this morning. Both he and Donner used the same word—evil companion."

Pete laughed (a little hysterically, I thought). The whole idea was ludicrous and we both knew it. Still, Pete said my being barred from the set was official. There was nothing else to do but pack and head back to Los Angeles.

As soon as I got home, I called Bob Hope and told him what had happened. "It's really a tribute," said Hope. "An evil companion for Jackie Gleason? I don't believe it. He makes you look like an altar boy. I don't believe it."

The cause of the banning was a lunch Jackie and I had before he was called to the set at 4 P.M. Jackie ordered his usual—six double Scotches with no ice, no soda, no water and no food. Jackie is very careful about drinking when he is working. He was told that all he was needed for in the late call were a few reaction shots with no dialogue. This is something any good actor can do even when comatose.

But Donner instead strapped him into a golf cart and had him drive around a huge Southern plantation chasing Pryor. Jackie drove the golf cart right into a swimming pool, a scene that turned out to be one of the funniest in the movie. Of course, I hadn't ordered Jackie's lunch, although I kept up with him the best I could. I got blamed for everything, however.

Jackie and I have been friends for over thirty-six years. We first met in 1949, when he came out to Hollywood to do "The Life of Riley," one of the very first television situation comedies. For six years prior to its television debut, it had been one of radio's most popular shows, starring the late William Bendix. Bendix, under contract to RKO Pictures, wasn't allowed to do the television version; in the early days of TV, movie studios were threatened by the new medium. Most studios barred all contract players from appearing on television, and many of them wouldn't even allow a TV set on the lot.

Gleason, a relatively unknown nightclub comedian at the time, was signed at six hundred dollars a week to replace Bendix on TV. That sounds like big money for those days, and it was. But there was one catch: Gleason couldn't live on six hundred a night, let alone six hundred a week. Jackie used to spend that much every night at the old Villa Capri on McCadden Place in the heart of Hollywood.

For Jackie, every night was New Year's Eve at the Villa Capri. Jackie was such a big spender that even his pal Frank Sinatra, a big spender himself, was impressed. Owner Patsy D'Amore, a vaudeville veteran, had given Jackie signing privileges.

When Jackie drank, everybody drank—and Jackie

□

signed the tab for the house. Every place I have ever gone with Jackie over the years, flush or broke, he has had signing privileges. Owners always know that somehow, sometime, he will pay them back in full—and then some.

Jackie only did one season of "Riley" and then he went back to New York. Patsy was left with an unpaid tab of five thousand bucks. To Patsy's credit, he never dunned Jackie for it. Nor did he ever seem to worry about it.

"He's gonna pay some day," said Patsy, in his thick Italian accent.

Three years passed, and in 1952, Gleason was the biggest thing on television, with an eleven-million-dollar contract from CBS-TV. Jackie came back to Hollywood for a vacation; he stayed at the posh Bel-Air Hotel. First night in town, he instructed his limousine driver to make the relatively long trek into Hollywood—and the Villa Capri.

He had invited a few friends, a small group compared to the old days, to have dinner with him at Patsy's. The tab for the pasta and vino could not have been more than seventy-five dollars.

Came time to depart and Gleason called Patsy over and asked once again for the pen. You could tell by the expression on Patsy's face that he thought the five-thousand-dollar tab was going to go higher. No need to worry. Gleason wrote out a check for six thousand dollars and handed it to Patsy.

"I'm a big tipper, pal," said Jackie as he handed Patsy the check in a sweeping gesture. Patsy almost screamed his thanks. The old tab had been paid—and with close to a thousand dollars interest.

▪ HOW SWEET IT IS ▪

·1·
A
STAR
IS
BORN

The year was 1916. The voices of the young Irish couple, loud in argument, echoed down the hallways of the tenement on Herkimer Street in Brooklyn, its walls scribbled with the ethnic graffiti of the Irish and Italian kids who lived there.

A dumbwaiter that provided an open shaft from the fourth floor to the janitor in the basement now resounded with their warring words. And to make matters worse, a wide-open air shaft midway in the tenement, much bigger than the dumbwaiter, made damn sure that everybody there knew that Herb and Mae Kelly Gleason were having one hell of a fight.

Fights among couples, both young and old, happened every day in these railroad flats of the Bushwick section.

□

No novelty, but this one was different. The Gleasons were fighting over something that most couples settle with loving words—the naming of a new baby boy.

Herb, a proud father, insisted that his son, born February 26, 1916, be named after him. Mae, Irish eyes blazing, argued that no child of hers would ever be called Herb, although she had married a man with that name. She wanted the boy named John, after the saint who wrote one of the Gospels.

The father countered that he had put up no argument when she named an older son, now a sickly boy of eleven, after Clement the First, fourth pope of the Roman Catholic Church and a saint to boot. For some reason, never quite known, Mae had called the older boy Clemence.

It was a fierce and a long argument, lasting three weeks. Herb finally won on paper. The birth certificate read Herbert John Gleason but no one, not even the father, ever called the boy Herb. His mother called him Jackie and she made sure that everyone else called him that, even her husband.

Today, Jackie Gleason doesn't know why his mother fought so against naming him Herb, but he's glad she did. Perhaps, with America soon to enter World War I, his mother thought Herbert sounded too Germanic. For whatever reason, Jackie Gleason looks better on a marquee. Maybe Mae knew what she was doing back there in 1916.

Jackie came into this world as a beautiful chubby boy with a full head of coal-black hair and sparkling blue eyes, thus qualifying him to be a full-fledged member of the Black Irish. He could have passed—except for the blue eyes—for the offspring of Mexican or Puerto Rican parents had there been any in the neighborhood. There weren't.

Jackie, as a Black Irish, came by his Latin look quite naturally. It was the heritage of his father mostly, who was born in the seaport city of Cork in Ireland, and of his mother, who came from county Kilkenny, inland in the Emerald Isle. Back in the Elizabethan Era, Sir Francis Drake, as admiral in the Queen's Navy, sank the Spanish Armada off the coasts of Ireland. The Irish were, then as now, fiercely Catholic and even more anti-British. The Spanish sailors who made it to shore were hidden by the Irish and were eventually absorbed into the Celtic population. Hence the Black Irish, those with black hair and blessed with such Irish-Latin names as Joyce or Costello.

The Bushwick section of Brooklyn was mostly poor Irish, along with poor Italians and poor Jews. Everybody was in a continual struggle for survival. Jackie's dad made twenty-five bucks a week, better than most of his neighbors.

"I don't ever remember starving," Jackie recalls. "But even so, the only thing my parents ever fought over was money. There never was enough to go around."

Most of the Gleason wages went for two things— tonics to keep young Clemence alive, and booze for Herb and Mae.

Clemence, sickly from birth, finally died at age fourteen, when Jackie was only three. He has little memory of his older brother. Clemence's death had a strange effect on Mae. She clung to Jackie as if he were her only possession in the world and, in a way, he was. The old man had a bad habit of losing himself in Prohibition speakeasies.

"My Mom kept me in the house all the time. I could never go out on the street and play with the other kids. I used to watch them with my face pressed against the window. I think this is how I developed my Poor Soul look. Hell, I didn't even start school until I was eight years old, two years older than the other kids in my class."

Cousin Renée Wilbert, daughter of Mae's older sister, Maggie, confirms this. A few years older than Jackie, she

□

3

was the one who walked him to school when the truant officer finally got him there. (Renée is the widow of the famous jockey Nick Wall, a favorite at Belmont and other New York tracks.)

Jackie was an obedient child. His mother wanted him in the house and that's where he stayed. Sometimes his father would take him to a Saturday matinee at the Halsey Theater in the neighborhood. There he saw his early idols, Charlie Chaplin and Buster Keaton, in two-reel silent comedies.

The Halsey also had five or six acts of vaudeville on the bill, and that's what intrigued the little boy the most. Once he stood up in the Halsey while a comedian was performing. He couldn't have been more than seven at the time. Jackie turned his back to the stage and saw all the people laughing their heads off. His father made him sit down but not before the little kid told his father he could do what that guy up there on the stage was doing.

His father laughed, not knowing, of course, that his son had just made one of the great theatrical prophecies.

Those Saturday matinees gave Jackie a break from his in-house imprisonment, but even more importantly, the matinees inspired him. With little else to do but look out the window, he started imitating the comic moves of Chaplin and Keaton, especially Buster Keaton. Gleason still thinks that Keaton is the greatest comic who ever lived, and he still uses many of the moves developed in his childhood.

Jackie remembers a little peculiarity about his father at those Saturday matinees. Before he went into the theater, his father always stopped in a store for a moment or two, leaving Jackie outside on the pavement. Whatever his father bought in the store was consumed on the premises because he never came out carrying any packages. It didn't

□
4

take the kid long to figure out that the store was just a front for a speakeasy and the old man had a snort or two before the matinee.

Even his mother had a set routine for drinking. She would complain to Jackie that her teeth hurt and that she was going to the dentist, and then, when she came home a little wobbly, she would say to Jackie, "It's the gas the dentist gives you. It makes you dizzy." Even in his pre-school days, Jackie would put his mother to bed, saying, "I know, Mom."

What he knew was that Mom also had visited a speakeasy, the same as Pop. "No wonder I have the thirst," he says now.

About the time Jackie started school, in 1924, Herb's pay was raised to thirty-five dollars a week, a good living wage then. Herb's brother was a big gun in the insurance company over in Manhattan where Herb worked, and it was his brother who had gotten Herb the job, and also the raise.

But it made no difference at home. Herb and Mae still argued over money and Herb had to supplement his income by selling candy on the job. Jackie remembers his father coming home with huge cans of peanuts, which Jackie and his mother had to bag for Herb to sell at a nickel apiece.

Jackie often lay in bed at night listening to his mother and father argue about money. Mae was a woman with great style who loved to dress well. She loved to party, too. Often she had friends in for laughs over a few bottles of bathtub gin (that's how most of it was made during Prohibition—by mixing straight alcohol and juniper berries in the bathtub). There's a lot of Mae in the Jackie Gleason of today.

Despite her love of bathtub gin, Mae Gleason was an

exceptional mother who did much to educate Jackie. She taught him how to read, and when he finally did go to school at age eight, he was far more advanced in reading than the other kids in PS 73.

Being Irish, Mae was well versed in the lore of her homeland, an island that was producing saints and scholars at a time when the rest of northern Europe, except for some monastic outposts, was barbaric. She made Jackie proud of his Irish heritage. More importantly, she instilled in her son a voracious appetite for reading, one he still has today.

Mae, considerably younger than Herb, was only fifteen when she married. Herb had a good ten years on her. She was the youngest child of five of an Irish sign painter. Being the youngest, she was the most spoiled and expected the same treatment from Herb. She didn't get it.

Herb came from a family considered well-to-do, and his people frowned on his marriage to the pretty Irish girl. Cousin Renée has no doubt that family pressure was behind an event in Jackie's life that was to leave a tragic and permanent scar. Jackie recalls:

"I was about nine when one day my pop didn't come home. A few days before, my mom and he had a violent argument and he took every picture out of the house that had him in it. That should have been the tip-off, but I was too young to know."

The day was December 15, 1925. Now Jackie was used to his dad staying away from home. Herb's usual custom was to pick up his paycheck on a Friday and then spend the weekend in a speakeasy on a binge. He usually drank double Manhattans until the money got low, then he drank home-brewed beer with an alcoholic content of around 23 percent.

In those days, closing laws weren't observed in speak-

□

easies. Hell, they weren't supposed to be open in the first place, so it was easy for a guy to drink around the clock. And Herb often did. As soon as he didn't come home to dry out for work, Mae hit all his favorite speakeasies. No Herb.

Jackie stayed up until she got home. "Where's Pop?" he asked.

"I don't know. I don't know," said the worried mother.

Jackie and Mae never saw Herb again. Cousin Renée recalls that Herb's family didn't really seem all that concerned about Herb's disappearance. His brother even issued an order at the insurance company where both brothers worked that the employees should not discuss it.

"We always figured that his family was scared of his drinking and wanted him away from Mae," says Cousin Renée. We thought maybe they had sent him down to South America or some other place just to get him out of town. They were behind his disappearance, I'm sure of that."

Whatever the reason, Herb's disappearance had a devastating effect on Jackie and his mother. It happened in the heart of the Christmas season. Jackie remembers it as the worst Christmas he ever had. No presents. No tree. No Pop.

"On Christmas Eve, Mom and I went to midnight mass at Our Lady of Lourdes Church. I prayed that Pop was still alive—and that he would come back to us. I was scared to death."

Herb's sudden departure, for whatever reason, left his wife destitute. She didn't even have what was left of his paycheck. And although Herb worked for an insurance firm, he didn't have a policy on himself.

The tragedy had a peculiar effect on Jackie, one that hounds him to this day. It left him with an appetite border-

□

ing on gluttony. He started craving food at all hours of the day or night. It also made him eat food fast, fearful that it would disappear as his father had. The psychiatrists tell you people who think the world has given them a rotten deal often eat to compensate.

(Marilyn Gleason does all the cooking for Jackie in their Lauderhill, Florida, home but she admits she can't cope with Jackie's desire to eat at 2 A.M. Down in Baton Rouge, during the filming of *The Toy,* the Baton Rouge Hilton provided Jackie with the first twenty-four-hour room service in the history of Baton Rouge.)

In his youth, that enormous appetite never seemed to bother him. He was a slender, handsome boy—very attractive to girls in the neighborhood (the Gleasons moved often from tenement to tenement but never out of the Bushwick neighborhood, nor out of the PS 73 school district). The ravenous appetite would catch up with Jackie, however, as the money got more plentiful and he became big on television. His fans would see him gain a hundred pounds from the Dumont days, when he started at 180, to the CBS-TV heyday, when he checked in sometimes at 280 pounds.

Herb's disappearance was especially tough on Jackie's mother. Too often, the police would come by their flat late at night and ask her to come down to the morgue and look at some stiff hauled from the river. Fortunately, it was never Herb.

Once a ray of hope came when one of the girls at the insurance company said she saw Herb shoveling snow on the street with a bunch of Bowery derelicts. Some of his men friends checked it out, but it wasn't Herb.

Jackie heard no more about his father until the mid-fifties, when he was already a big star on television and forty years old. The FBI came to him with word that his father had died in Connecticut at age seventy-six. Jackie

□

gave it some credence at first because he knew his father's people came from Connecticut, but, in the next breath, the FBI asked him to do a benefit for them. That more or less queered that.

"I remember thinking when they first told me he had died, if he had only dropped by once to say hello. Surely, he must have seen me on TV. Everybody else in the country did. I never was angry about Pop leaving us. I figured there must be something between him and Mom that I didn't know about. He always was okay with me. He had a great sense of humor, that I do remember. If he had just dropped by once. Just once."

Mae was too proud to take relief, as welfare assistance was called in those days, although she was deserving of it. Instead, she took a job as a token clerk on the subway that ran between Brooklyn and Manhattan—the BMT. It was a tough job working in that cage, unheated in winter and sweltering in summer. Jackie remembers his mother going to work in winter with blankets she could wrap around her legs.

"All the other guys in our block used to play a game jumping over the turnstile to beat the BMT out of a nickel. I couldn't do it, knowing what my mom went through on that job."

When Jackie first started going to school at age eight, the other kids used to laugh at him and he couldn't understand why. Finally, he discovered that he was speaking with his mother's Irish brogue, practically the only sound of language he heard at home.

Like most of the Irish, Mae dropped her *h*'s. She said "I t'ink" instead of "I think" or "I t'ought" instead of "I thought." Jackie did the same at school. And, since he was Irish, he opened his mouth plenty at school, arguing with his teachers. Exceptionally well read, even as a child, he argued every point with them. By his own admission, he was a smart-assed kid in school.

And Jackie was the same way on the street. When he had been locked up in that flat, he'd studied all the other kids in the street. He knew who could fight and who couldn't. He knew who would jump and who wouldn't. He had the whole neighborhood cased before he ever got out of the house. That house imprisonment would make most kids introverted. It made Jackie just the opposite—cocky as hell.

This same cockiness almost cost Jackie his show-business debut. When the time came for his eighth-grade graduation play, the teachers, fed up with him in class, passed him over for the show. Jackie went over their heads and auditioned for the principal in his office. He did Little Red Riding Hood in a Yiddish accent and had the principal rolling over his desk. He ordered that Jackie not only be in the play but be master of ceremonies as well.

The graduation show, an academic amateur night, also marked the debut of the Gleason ad-lib-insult humor. Someone knocked over the mike during the show and the principal picked it up and set it right.

"That's the first thing you have ever done for this school," ad-libbed Jackie. Even the principal thought it was funny. It doesn't sound like much today, but that night in 1932, it was a regular riot, as Ralph Kramden might say.

"I met my first critic that night—my mom. She said I was good but too damn fresh. She was probably right."

▪ 2 ▪
FROM
POOL
HUSTLER
TO
COMIC

The last thing Mae Gleason wanted to do was pull Jackie out of high school. Jackie, somewhat fed up with school, offered no objection when a relative told the principal of Bushwick High that the six-teen-year-old boy was the sole support of his mother. He spent another few weeks at a trade high school, but in all, Jackie had only about a month of high school education.

Mae's dream had always been for Jackie to complete high school and then go to college—with the Jesuits, per-haps, at Fordham.

Mae, while still a fairly young woman—only in her for-ties—had lost a son, a husband and all her dreams. She had a tough enough time keeping Jackie and herself alive, let alone sending him through high school and college. There was just too damn much poverty in that little flat.

Life got to be too much for her, and her drinking increased. She tried as best she could to hide this defeated state from her beloved Jackie, but the kid was too smart for that.

"All that tragedy made her a loner," Cousin Renée recalls. "Jackie was all she had in life—all she lived for. Thank God, he always was a good boy."

Jackie himself doesn't look back on those days as unhappy ones. "My mother was a remarkable woman, even with all the odds stacked against her. We might not have had a nickel in the house some days, but there was always plenty of love. We were very lonely without Pop. Sometimes, I think we should have talked more about Pop's leaving us. We never did. I wish now that we had."

Jackie will tell you that hardly a day goes by, even now, when he doesn't think of his mother struggling to make ends meet in that little railroad flat. He proudly remembers the day he brought home his confirmation certificate, circa 1929. He was number one in his class at Our Lady of Lourdes.

"I can still see her folding it after looking at it a long time. Then she pressed it between the pages of her prayer book, the missal of the mass. I knew she was very proud of me at that very moment. She was a good Irish Catholic mother."

Jackie was good to his mother, but by no means was he a complete angel. Like many kids of his era, whether in Brooklyn or wherever, he frequented the neighborhood poolroom. It was mild by today's standards, where kids are into heavy sex and drugs in junior high school, but back in the twenties and thirties, poolrooms were looked upon by most people as a nonstop ticket to hell.

□

To help out at home, Jackie got a job racking up balls in a poolroom when he was only ten. He didn't tell his mother, but she found out. One day, she came marching into the poolroom looking for him, but Jackie was under the table, hiding on a freshly oiled floor.

He kept the job all through elementary school—and it was an experience that would prove invaluable to him in later life. The job carried little pay, but all the free pool he could shoot. By age twelve, Jackie could beat anyone who came into the poolroom—man, woman or hustler. The owner of the poolroom backed him against all comers. Jackie made more money beating all comers than he did racking up balls.

His pals even did better. One hocked his father's Sunday go-to-meeting suit and bet it all on Jackie. Fortunately, the old man was a cop and didn't miss the suit on a weekday. The kid won ten bucks on Jackie and redeemed the old man's suit with no one the wiser. Total profit—five bucks.

Of course, grown men didn't like it when they found they had been hustled by a kid, and there were plenty of fights. Now, you might think the first impulse in a poolroom fight is to swing a cue.

"Not so," says Jackie. "You throw the balls. That will stop a fight quick."

Jackie's sole Academy Award nomination would come in 1961, when he played Minnesota Fats in *The Hustler,* with Paul Newman and George C. Scott. Gleason needed no stunt pool players, as the other actors did. And in 1982, he played a con man in *The Sting II* at Universal. In preparation for a difficult afternoon's shooting in a poolroom scene with Karl Malden, Jackie had his usual six-double-Scotch lunch.

Jennings Lang, the producer, had allotted two days for

this supposedly difficult scene, in which Gleason bets a thousand dollars that he can beat Malden the best out of five in banking balls up and down the table into a corner pocket. Lang figured that all the stunt pool-playing would take time; he apparently wasn't aware that Gleason shoots pool like Willie Mosconi.

Malden, with the help of an expert pool double, missed the first of the five shots, per script, then pocketed the next four straight.

"Four out of five, beat that!" shouted the exuberant Malden to Gleason.

Gleason chalked his cue with the flourish of a Reggie Van Gleason the Third and then turned to the cameraman and said, "Shoot me full. I want the camera to see my ball hit the other ball from overhead as soon as it leaves my cue, then follow the shot all the way until it comes back into this corner pocket. That way, the audience will know that The Great Gleason needs no stunt man."

Jackie banked the first four balls smoothly up and down the table, back into the corner pocket. On the fifth and decisive shot, he was Reggie again as he chalked his cue. Wonders of wonders, he departed from the script and executed a triple bank shot, something that a trick-shot artist might do. The ball plunked neatly into the same corner pocket.

The happy director yelled, "Print it!" Producer Lang was in ecstasy. Happiness is a Hollywood producer who has just seen a two-day shooting schedule come in in a half-hour.

Skill was the best thing Jackie got from hanging around that Brooklyn poolroom. Otherwise, it was an impecunious living at best.

Show business, not pool, was Jackie's consuming passion in life. The applause and laughs he got at that eighth-

□

14

grade graduation show had set him up for life. When he wasn't in the poolroom, he had the other kids in the neighborhood rolling with laughter on the street corners of Bushwick. He was a naturally funny kid.

Phil Foster, who played Laverne De Fazio's father in "Laverne and Shirley," remembers those old days.

"Jackie must have been around sixteen or so. I know he had quit school, as that was the legal age. We all entered amateur contests at the Bushwick Theater. He bombed like the rest of us but he kept trying, and before long, he was doing amateur contests at the Halsey."

Now the Halsey was the same theater where Jackie's father used to take him on Saturday matinees to see Buster Keaton, Charlie Chaplin and live vaudeville acts. Jackie got so good in the amateur contests that the manager asked him to be master of ceremonies. Sammy Birch, the paid emcee, was leaving to try the big time in New York. Birch, not that much older than Jackie, took the Irish kid under his wing and taught him the tricks of the master-of-ceremonies trade. Jackie later found out it was Birch who had pitched Jackie to take over his spot.

When Birch left, Jackie took over at four dollars a night. It wasn't an every-night job; twice a week at best. Jackie, who had never seen Milton Berle work, was doing the same thing at the Halsey that Berle was doing on Broadway as a headliner. Jackie sang, danced and kidded around with the other acts. He also did impressions, but he was no Rich Little in those days.

This was all happening around 1933—the year of Repeal—and Jackie was supplementing his Halsey income with bar mitzvahs, birthday parties and so on around the neighborhood. He even teamed up with another kid in his gang, named Charlie Cretter. The two of them came up with an act. The format was old, even in those days, but it

□

15

was surefire. In burlesque, they still call it "Man in the Box." While one guy goes onstage first, the other heckles, usually from a theatrical box. Often, he does it from the back of the audience. (Phil Cook and His Four Hawaiians, Phil Baker, and Ted Healy and His Stooges were vaudeville headliners of that era who used variations of the format. Healy took his Stooges with him when Hollywood called and they later became world-famous on their own as The Three Stooges, after Healy's death. One of Cook's four Hawaiians left the act when it played the Orpheum in Los Angeles and decided to open a chili parlor. It was the late Dave Chasen, and that chili parlor today is the renowned Chasen's restaurant, a famous eating place for the Hollywood crowd and President Ronald Reagan's favorite when in Beverly Hills.)

For their wardrobe, Gleason and Cretter borrowed tuxedos from another pal whose father belonged to the Masons, a lodge that often requires much black-tie dress. One of the tuxedos was in contemporary style, the other was something out of Diamond Jim Brady, complete with brocade vest. Gleason chose that one, of course. Cretter and Gleason had use of the tuxedos as long as there were no formal Masonic gatherings.

Their act today would get booed off the stage, but back in 1933, it was funny. For example, Cretter would get onstage, apologizing for the non-show of his partner. He had no idea what had happened to him. Embarrassed, he would turn to the orchestra leader and say, "Play me an air."

This was Gleason's cue to stroll through the audience, yelling in a Yiddish accent, "If you sing, you will get the air." Corny, yes. A Henny Youngman reject, but it went over big in Brooklyn, where Jewish audiences loved an Irish goy doing Yiddish. Once Jackie heard the laughs—

and the team got a lot of them in those semi-pro days—he was hooked for life.

Jackie's hardworking mother finally found a flat she liked at 328 Chauncey Street in the Bushwick section. It would be the last place where Jackie would live with her. (If you want an idea what the kitchen looked like, just watch a rerun of "The Honeymooners." Few people, outside of RALPH (Royal Association for Longevity and Preservation of The Honeymooners) know that 328 Chauncey Street is also the same address as that of Ralph and Alice Kramden.)

Mae and Jackie lived in a tenement called Dennehey's Flats. It was so called because it was managed, not owned, by Tom and Anna Dennehey from county Kerry. The Denneheys would prove good neighbors to the Gleasons.

Tom liked Jackie but thought he would never amount to more than a well-dressed pool hustler. Maybe that was because the Denneheys had a pretty daughter named Julie who was Jackie's first love when he was a teenager. Fathers always take a dim view of their daughters' first suitors. But old man Dennehey had a lasting effect on Jackie: He would always be the invisible customer at the bar in the Joe the Bartender sketches.

Jackie's romance with Julie lasted until he emceed a local talent show that featured two pretty ballerinas called the Halford Twins. They weren't really twins, just sisters, but they looked and dressed like twins. Their names were Genevieve and Geraldine.

The handsome Irish kid with the black wavy hair fell like a drunken sailor for Genevieve, who was about as radically different from Jackie as any girl could be. But what difference does that make when you are both seventeen and in love?

Genevieve was extremely pious, while Jackie, at some

urging from his mother, was halfheartedly religious. Genevieve went to mass and communion almost daily. She prayed for all the souls in purgatory, but when she met Jackie, she started praying for him most of all. His rough street language shocked her. Worse, she didn't think him the least bit funny and never laughed at his jokes. For most comedians, that would have been the ultimate kiss-off. But despite all this odd-couple matching, Jackie really fell for Genevieve and she, inexplicably, fell for him.

"Don't ask me why," Jackie says today. "I would have made a good hoodlum and Gen a good nun."

Gen was the good and pure girl that every Irish youth in Brooklyn wants to marry, and Jackie was the street rowdy every good and pure girl wants to reform. Marriage, however, was a long way off. As an amateur-show emcee, Jackie was making no more than four bucks a night, and only a few nights a week at that.

Jackie's new love for Genevieve gave him a new discipline. He worked harder and even hired two "writers," paying them out of his meager earnings. The writers were two ushers at Loew's Metropolitan, which featured big-time acts like Berle and Eddie Garr, an actor-comedian well known in vaudeville. (Years later, when he worked with her in *Sting II,* Jackie found out that actress Teri Garr was Eddie's daughter.)

The ushers did very little writing, but they were expert at copying down Berle's jokes. Jackie was thus stealing from Berle at a time when other comedians were accusing Berle of stealing from them. Walter Winchell, the powerful Broadway columnist, had already dubbed Milton "The Thief of Bad Gags." In those days, every act stole from all the others, but Berle got rapped because he would steal a joke and do it better. That was a violation of the comedians' code.

□

When the Halsey audience heard Jackie doing Berle's act, they thought he was the funniest man they had ever heard. Most of the people who went to the Halsey couldn't afford the prices at Loew's Metropolitan. Once someone in the neighborhood must have robbed a bank, because he went over to Manhattan and caught Milton at Loew's State. He came back and told Jackie that Milton Berle had stolen his act.

Amateur nights were not the only jobs that Jackie got in those days. He also emceed auto thrill shows, getting laughs while cars were smashing all over the place, just as he later would with Burt Reynolds in the popular *Smokey and the Bandit* movies.

And he worked for a while as a comic diver in a tank act, where he'd dive off a twenty-foot platform into a tank that looked about as big as a wet towel. Jackie soon discovered that the trick was to grease the tank and himself; that way he would slide in and slip out.

Tank diving was a fun occupation as long as the show played around Staten Island and Brooklyn, sometimes Coney Island. When it went on the road, Mae demurred. She didn't want her son, not yet eighteen, to leave home. She still clung to him. It was a big decision for Jackie, but the star diver showed up drunk one night and made it easy. The impresario asked Jackie to take his place, which meant a dive from a sixty-foot tower into a tank that looked like a coffee cup from that height. Jackie closed his eyes and dived, but that scary experience ended his diving career. He stayed home with his mother.

Gleason even took a fling at boxing in small clubs around Brooklyn. Prize money was five bucks, and Jackie always cooked up a scheme with his opponent to take it easy with the punches, and afterwards they would split the money evenly. This worked okay until Jackie met up with

□

an honest fighter who refused to pull his punches. He beat
the hell out of Jackie. (Years later, the fellow visited Jackie
backstage at CBS-TV after a television show. Jackie: "I
showed him the scar I still carry from that fight.")

Although Jackie was getting paid for his work at the
Halsey, little as it was, he still considered himself in the
amateur ranks. And he was. He knew that staying in
Brooklyn meant staying in the small time. The big time was
only a river away, but it might as well have been a con-
tinent.

It took a major tragedy to propel Jackie across that
river. In the summer of 1934, his mother developed a nasty
carbuncle on her neck. Up until this thing hit her, she had
been as full of life as her impoverished state would allow.
She still thought Herb would show up again, despite the
misgivings of her sisters and Cousin Renée, and life would
go on as before.

As the carbuncle grew bigger, the pain got worse.
Jackie noticed a big difference in his mother. Where once
she had loved to dress up and go out and have a few laughs
with the girls, or else have friends over for some gin, she
now spent most of her time on a couch in the living room,
and suffered in silence.

Every day, Jackie would beg and plead with his
mother to have a doctor look at that ugly sore, but she had
no use for doctors. She was Irish and stubborn. Once, un-
beknownst to Mae, Anna Dennehey called a nearby hospital and said there was an emergency at the Gleason flat.
Mae all but kicked the intern out. She wouldn't let him
look at her carbuncle. There was nothing for the young
doctor to do but walk away.

Jackie was up against the wall. His only recourse was
to buy every salve and painkiller the druggest recom-

mended. None of them did any good, so Jackie just kept up his daily pleading for his mother to see a doctor.

In those pre-air-conditioning days, the sore made a terrible stench. But even then, Mae would not budge on her no-doctor ultimatum. One night, the stench got so bad and the pain so violent, that Jackie, with Julie Dennehey's help, put a match to a needle to sterilize it and himself tried to lance the carbuncle. He tried and tried but he couldn't do it. It needed a doctor's scalpel. Mae suffered into the spring of 1935.

One night, Jackie started to go down to the corner hangout with some of the boys, but a sudden instinct made him stay home. Julie and some of his friends stayed with him, playing cards in the living room.

His mother's moaning, worse than usual, made some of the gang want to leave, but Jackie urged them to stay. They all did.

"We kept on with the card game and then, suddenly, Mom's groans turned to gasps. It was just like that. I had never seen anyone die before, but I knew that final gasp, which rattled, was the final one."

Jackie went over to the couch and felt his mother's forehead. It was cold. He knew she was dead but didn't want to admit it. He asked Julie to call a doctor to make sure.

It only took a cursory examination on the doctor's part until he gave it to Jackie tersely: "Your mother's dead of erysipelas."

Jackie didn't know what erysipelas was, and even if he had, he was too shocked to react. (Erysipelas, to simplify, is an acute inflammation of the skin that ultimately destroys the red blood cells, as it did in Mae's case. This cell destruction brings on anemia—and death.)

The memory of that night is still with Jackie.

"I walked into my bedroom and sat on the edge of the bed and started crying like I was having convulsions. I couldn't stop. I knew I had lost everything I had in the world—my mom."

In retrospect, Jackie wishes he hadn't been such an obedient son. If he had been a tough son of a bitch, he would have carried his mother screaming and kicking to the hospital. Instead, he respected her wishes and he has been sorry ever since.

Cousin Renée and her mother Maggie, Mae's older sister, came over to the house soon after Mae died.

"Her face was swollen and the inflammation was still there. Jackie was always a good boy. He did everything he could for his mother. He tried to get her to see a doctor. We all did, but she just wouldn't be budged. She just had a thing against all doctors, and none of us could shake her on it. It finally killed her.

"I remember when she first got the carbuncle, she ordered a couch on time from a furniture company. She spent months on that couch, and then when she died, the store repossessed it before we could burn it. The doctor told us to burn everything that Mae had come in contact with, but every stick of furniture in that house was repossessed before poor Mae was cold in the ground."

Today, Jackie finds it hard to believe that he had turned nineteen when his mother died on April 12, 1935. He recalls feeling much younger at the time, probably because of his closeness to his mother. But the cemetery records, which Renée still has, authenticate the exact date of death.

With his mother gone, Jackie was all alone in the world—and still a teenager. Oh, sure, he had aunts and uncles and Cousin Renée, six years older and married. But it was the Depression, and they all had enough problems of their own.

The Denneheys were like family, too, and good-hearted. They couldn't do enough for Jackie after his mother died.

There was no insurance, which meant that Mae would have to be buried in potter's field, the biblical term for a pauper's graveyard. How she would have hated that. But, miracle of miracles, when the folks at the BMT heard of their former co-worker's death, they collected two hundred and fifty dollars to bury her. Thank God for the BMT.

Jackie had no money, but Aunt Maggie gave him five dollars to buy flowers for his mother's coffin—"From your loving son, Jackie."

It rained the day of his mother's funeral, but all the neighbors, relatives and friends who loved her turned out in force for the low-requiem mass at Our Lady of Lourdes Church. She was buried in the Gate of Heaven Cemetery in Brooklyn. Afterward, everybody came back to the Denneheys for some drinks and food.

"Then we all sat out on the Denneheys' stoop for a while," Jackie recalls. "Mr Dennehey asked me to move in with them until I got on my feet. I thanked him but said I was going to New York and make it on my own as a comedian. I didn't tell him I only had thirty-six cents to my name. If I had, he probably wouldn't have let me go—or else given me money he could ill afford."

Jackie's next step was to con the cleaner out of the only suit he owned. He promised to pay later—and he eventually did.

"I knew no fear. I was stupid, brash, arrogant and broke. I headed for the subway with my thirty-six cents but couldn't bring myself to jump over the turnstile, after all my mother had gone through for me. I paid my five cents.

"As I rode that subway to the Times Square Station, I kept thinking that my mother was buried on her fiftieth birthday, and it was the first time since I was a baby that I hadn't scraped up enough money to buy her a present."

· 3 ·
JACKIE GLEASON, BOY COMIC

It's tough to be an orphan at age nineteen. It's even tougher if you are an orphan in the world's largest city with only thirty-one cents in your pocket.

Such a state of affairs might have scared the hell out of anyone else. But fear was not a word in Jackie's dictionary. What was important to him was that an amateur comedian had made it across the river from Brooklyn to the big time in Manhattan.

Like any other out-of-towner, Jackie strolled through the Times Square theatrical district gawking at the marquees. He felt a certain kinship with the big names up there, even though he was broke and they were successful.

Over at the Capitol, he saw Bob Hope's name in big

electric lights. Hope, hot after his Broadway musical hit in *Roberta,* was headlining a show that featured singer Dolores Reade, who was also Mrs. Hope.

On the other side of the square, at Loew's State, Milton Berle was the headliner for an all-comedy show that featured Frank and Milt Britton and their crazy band; Ben Blue, best of the Charlie Chaplin imitators; Ballantine, a magician who never finished one trick, and, of course, Henny Youngman, a onetime Brooklyn printer who was billed as King of the One-Liners. "That's because he can't remember the second line," Berle would quip onstage.

Besides being broke and orphaned, Jackie didn't know a single soul in Manhattan. Oh, there was Sammy Birch, the young comic who had helped Jackie at the Halsey with the amateur shows, teaching him all the tricks of emceeing. But Sammy had left Brooklyn for Manhattan the year before, and no one, least of all Jackie, had ever heard from him again. No one had been able to tell Jackie how to get in touch with Sammy.

However, none of this crossed Jackie's mind as he strolled through the crowded streets of Times Square. What did nag at him was that he was hungry. He stopped at one of the stands so popular in those days that sold waffles with apple butter and sweet cider. The waffle with apple butter cost a nickel, and so did the cider.

Munching his waffle and sipping his cider, Jackie watched the Times Square regulars amble by. Suddenly, he spotted Sammy Birch. Ten million people in the city and he spotted the only guy he knew! Waffle and cider in hand, Jackie ran after Birch, yelling "Sammy!" at the top of his lungs.

Sammy was sorry to hear that Jackie's mother had died. He'd known and loved her as had all in the old neighborhood. Sammy asked Jackie only one question: "Have you got a place to stay?"

Jackie's twenty-one cents would not have bought a bed even in the worst Bowery flophouse, so he moved in with Sammy and another comic named Walter Wayne at the Hotel Maxwell on West Forty-ninth Street. The rent was six dollars a week, and Sammy carried Jackie until he could get on his feet. It was a kind gesture on Sammy's part, and Jackie never forgot it. When Jackie hit it big on television, Sammy always had work on the Gleason show.

As for food, the comics solved breakfast by sleeping past it. A café around the corner had a daily special for either forty-nine or fifty-nine cents, depending upon the entrée. Whoever had the money for the meal got the entrée. The others ate soup or salad, sometimes dessert. And Jackie soon learned the survival trick known to all starving actors in those New York days, "potage à la Automat." The Automat had hot water—free—in a spigot for tea. Bowls also were available without charge. You'd take a bowlful of hot water and then add catsup, Tabasco and A-1 steak sauces and a little salt and pepper, all of which were on the table. Stir, and you had an almost tasty tomato soup. To go with it, there were always untouched rolls and bread left on a plate by a dieting shopgirl. The price was right, and it kept Jackie away from the Salvation Army soup kitchens.

Sammy Birch was a friend in more ways than one. He came home one night and told Jackie that a booker he knew, Solly Shaw, had a job for Jackie at Tiny's Chateau in Reading, Pennsylvania. It wasn't Broadway, or even off-Broadway, but it was work, at nineteen bucks a week for one week only, more money than Jackie had ever seen at one time. Solly advanced him the bus fare out of his com-

□

mission, and Jackie was on his way to his first job as a professional comedian.

On the way down to Reading, in the heart of Pennsylvania Dutch farming country, Jackie wondered if his brash Brooklyn act would go over with these people. He did something that he had never done before—and has never done since—he changed his act. He did a stand-up monologue and, since he was not yet Bob Hope or Frank Fay, he bombed. Oh, how he bombed at his first show.

The owner of Tiny's Chateau was on the phone immediately. Half the customers in the place gathered around to watch him drop the quarters in the pay phone. It was a big thing in those days to call New York from Reading.

"What the fuck do you mean sending me this punk kid?" the owner screamed at Solly Shaw. "He's about as funny as a dose of clap. He's fired after the midnight show!"

The owner, who had been fuming a moment before, then noticed the nineteen-year-old Jackie, standing with his Poor Soul look, and, feeling sorry for him, called, "Come over to the bar, kid. I'll buy you a drink."

Jackie recalls downing about fifteen Scotches. Came time for the second show, he was really loaded and didn't give a damn what happened. He was fired anyhow. He walked on stage thinking funny, he recalls, and said whatever came off the top of his head. He insulted Reading, the tavern owner and the customers. He did impressions and threw in a little singing and soft-shoe.

The customers howled, cheered and pounded on the tables. They couldn't get enough of this brilliant young comic.

The owner grabbed him. "Why the fuck didn't you do that act the first show? You're great!"

Jackie could only answer: "What act?"

□

Jackie had ad-libbed that second show and didn't exactly recall what he had done. Once again, the owner was dropping quarters into the phone as his customers watched. He got Solly out of bed at 2 A.M.

"Solly," he screamed, "forget that first call. This kid's a riot. I'm holding him over an extra week." No comic had ever been held over at Tiny's Chateau; here was Jackie establishing a record on his first professional engagement.

Jackie had one problem. He couldn't quite remember what he had done at that second show. There was only one thing to do—show up early the next night and drink his act back. It may have been that night that turned Jackie into a world-class drinker. If they had given Oscars for nightclub performances in Reading, Jackie, in his acceptance speech, would have had to thank J&B Scotch.

Solly Shaw, who had booked many comics into Tiny's Chateau, was delighted to have been responsible for the first ever to have been held over. After that, he found work for Jackie all over New Jersey, which had plenty of small clubs. Jackie worked the entire summer of 1935 at The Oasis at Budd Lake, a popular New Jersey resort. It was at Budd Lake that he savored his first taste of page-one publicity. Kiki Roberts, the gorgeous showgirl moll of gangster Jack "Legs" Diamond, couldn't swim. Jackie, who could, rescued her from drowning when she fell out of a boat. The New York tabloids splashed photos of hero Jackie and cheesecake shots of Kiki's famous body all over town.

"She couldn't have drowned with those boobs," Jackie recalls. Luckily for Jackie, Diamond had been conveniently bumped off earlier, so Jackie spent the remainder of the summer consoling Kiki. It was his first encounter with big-time sex, and only attracted more publicity. After that, Jackie's shows at The Oasis were Standing Room Only. That summer was a barrel of laughs for Jackie, onstage and

□

off. He had a beautiful showgirl on one side and in front of him was always a drink.

He still likes to drink, but never to excess when he's working. As the late great saloon comic Joe E. Lewis once said, "Some people drink to forget, Jackie Gleason and I drink to remember."

(Even now, after two triple bypass heart operations, Jackie will knock off six double Scotches for lunch, usually with no food. He vows he is no alcoholic.

"An alcoholic doesn't know why he drinks," he explains. "I do. I drink to get bagged, and besides, booze removes all warts and blemishes, not from you but from the broad you are drinking with. Waiter, more wart medicine.")

Work was plentiful for the young comic that summer and fall. But the big money eluded him. It seemed that wherever he worked, he got the same nineteen bucks a week. In those Depression days, it was good money for a kid who had no one but himself to support. But Jackie, ever the big spender, always found himself borrowing on his salary a week or two in advance, even with the free food and drink that came with the jobs.

The more he worked, the funnier he became. He developed a keen sense of timing. He knew how to keep his act moving by throwing in a song for the boys at the bar at closing time, or perhaps shuffling a time step or two between the jokes and impressions. He was perfecting all of the moves that would later make him famous on television. His idols were silent star Buster Keaton and the talkies' Jack Oakie, movie comedians who knew how to move. He also loved W. C. Fields, who never made a move that didn't produce a laugh.

Jackie played the little clubs all over New Jersey and even once made it to Alpena, Michigan. He finally wound

□
30

up at the Club Miami in Newark, only a cab ride away from the big time in Manhattan. The Club Miami was one of those places known in the trade as a "bucket-of-blood joint," catering to longshoremen and others on the Jersey waterfront. The customers dared you to be funny, and heckling was a way of life. For the performer, it was more important to throw a good punch than a punch line. Jackie would use all the standard anti-heckling lines, such as "Is that your face, sir, or did your pants fall down?" or "I never forget a face, but in your case, I'll make an exception." But occasionally, Jackie would have to invite a more persistent heckler out into the alley and beat the hell out of him.

The customers respected that. Jackie, a product of the Brooklyn streets, beat all comers—with one exception. A short, squat Italian, built like a beer barrel, came in one night and sat ringside. He kept drinking beer as fast as Budweiser could brew it, and he kept stepping on Jackie's punch lines. Jackie, furious, didn't even waste his bon mots on this guy; he invited him straight out into the alley.

George Sossin, owner of the Club Miami, tried to stop Jackie, warning him that this guy was tougher than all the others. Jackie, displaying no fear, brushed George aside and went out into the alley. The short guy threw just one punch, and Jackie woke up in the alley about an hour later, feeling as if he'd been hit by a Mack truck. Jackie had made the mistake of challenging "Two Ton" Tony Galento. Three years later, Galento would fight Joe Louis for the world's heavyweight title. In 1939, Joe finally knocked out the pot bellied fighter who trained on beer, but not before Galento clobbered Louis with the same punch he had used on Gleason.

"Tony taught me a valuable lesson," says Gleason. "Don't tangle with title contenders in a nightclub. Joe Louis once told me that no one had ever hit him as hard as Galento did."

□

· 4 ·
JACKIE
IN
LOVE

The Club Miami really was a tough joint. Milton Berle, when he first heard of a kid comic there who was stealing his act, visited the club to confront Gleason.

"The food was so bad at the Club Miami, the rats went next door to eat," says Milton.

In those days, Newark had a 4 A.M. closing time, but the Club Miami was throwing drunks in the gutter as late as 8 A.M. "The cops were afraid to go there," Jackie recalls. "All fights were settled—*pow*!—right in the kisser. I think that's where I first used that expression, little knowing that I would be saying it to Alice Kramden on 'The Honeymooners' someday."

Waiters didn't have to be union in the Club Miami;

□

better that they be Golden Gloves champions. George Sossin's idea of a good waiter was one who could throw a punch without spilling the drinks on the tray.

To Jackie, however, it was a fun place. He loved it so much, he used to spend all his afternoons there at the bar. He loved to listen to Sossin, always moaning about turning off the lights. Once, he ordered a waiter to go into a back room and turn off some lights. The waiter returned like Jesse Owens in the 1936 Olympics. "Them ain't no lights. The joint's on fire." Sure enough, it was, and the fire department came in minutes. That night the show went on as usual. To give you an idea of what a crumb-bum honky-tonk it was, some of the customers thought George had redecorated the place with scorched palm trees.

When Jackie first worked the Club Miami in 1936, he only worked weekends for his usual nineteen bucks. The club had been dying before Jackie was hired, but Gleason was a big draw. Before long he had the club's take up to eight hundred or a thousand dollars per night on week-ends—big money in those Depression years.

George, a smart businessman, wanted Jackie to work a full week, so Jackie asked for a raise to thirty dollars. When George wouldn't budge above twenty-five, Jackie started packing his props. Jackie got his thirty.

The job also came with free booze and food. The chef once told Sossin he would be better off paying Jackie two hundred a week and making him buy his own food. A typical between-shows snack for Gleason was three steaks, maybe a chicken or two, and a dozen Scotches neat. After all, he still was a growing boy.

People who frequented the club in those days all remember Gleason with fondness. Tony Zoppi, who later became entertainment director at the Riviera Hotel in Las Vegas, recalls:

"Jackie was *the* hot comedian in those days, not only in Newark but all over northern New Jersey. I was living nearby in Long Branch and we all were quoting Gleason or talking about what he did on the Club Miami stage."

It was no wonder that Jackie had a funny act; he was still getting all his material from the two ushers at Loew's Metropolitan, who were breaking their pencils copying down Berle's act. Milton, by this time, was the hot comic on Broadway, and he had a reputation wherever there were big-time vaudeville houses. Milton held the longevity record at Manhattan's Palace, the valhalla of all stars of vaudeville.

Milton heard about this kid in Newark doing all his jokes.

"I even went over to Newark, which to someone from Broadway was like making a trip to Chicago or Des Moines. I sat in the back of the Club Miami and watched Gleason work. He not only was doing my act; worse, he was funny. I went backstage and said, 'Hey, kid, you know you're doing my act?'

"He wasn't the least bit frightened, or apologetic. He just gave me that Gleason look. You know the sideways twisting of the head that everybody from Brooklyn does, especially when they talk. He said, 'Where did you get it, pallie?'

"He was brash, arrogant and cocky. I didn't get mad at him because, to tell the truth, I recognized a little of myself in him. So I said, 'Kid, it's okay to use that material in Newark, but if you ever get in the big time, steal from Youngman.'

"Jackie and I have had our differences over the years but we are friends. He has made me what I am today—unemployed."

Jackie's run at the Club Miami, with its customers who

□

3 5

dared a comic to be funny, gave him a kind of training that today's young comics can't get anywhere. It was a place to be bad onstage, where you could learn what works and what doesn't.

After Jackie had spent a few months at the Club Miami—this was early 1936—the owner of the Empire Burlesque Theater in Newark caught Gleason's act. He offered Jackie forty dollars a week to do four shows a day at the Empire. Jackie, making ten dollars less at the Club Miami, liked working there. He didn't want to leave. The burlesque owner said that was no problem, because he could handle both jobs easily. The first burlesque show went on at noon and the last one ended before he was due on the Miami floor. It was a long day but seventy bucks a week for both shows was big money, so he took the burlesque offer.

This period, around 1936 and 1937, was the heyday of burlesque comedy in America. And it is to burlesque that Jackie owes his greatest debt. Even Jackie's rivals will admit that he became television's greatest sketch comedian, and it was burlesque that gave him his doctorate in comedy sketches.

Jackie was the house comic at the Empire. The big-name burlesque comics—Phil Silvers, Rags Ragland, Abbott and Costello, and others—worked off a burlesque wheel, or circuit. It stretched from the Follies on Main Street in Los Angeles to Minsky's on Forty-second Street in New York, with big-city stops in between. The headline strippers also worked off the wheel. Only the house comics and a chorus line that as a rule couldn't dance were based at the local burlesque houses.

Traditionally, the wheel comic looked down on the house comic in a snobbish and spiteful way. And the traveling comics always came with their own straight men. The

strippers, usually gorgeous with knockout figures, always
worked in sketches with the wheel comics.

Jackie, as house comic, had none of these luxuries. He
didn't even work full-stage. His bits were called "olios" a
vaudeville term for acts performed in front of the curtain.
Worse, Jackie had no professional straight man, such as the
late Jack Albertson, who played straight for Phil Silvers in
burlesque. Jackie had to do his stuff with a tap dancer or a
juggler, which was like working with the Nuremberg Jury.
But Jackie was still funny, a fact which the traveling comics
all hated.

In burlesque, sketches are never rehearsed. Every
comic, road or house, knows every sketch by heart. For
instance, the headline comic might say, "We're doing
Niagara Falls" (one of the more famous of burlesque routines in which the comic goes berserk every time he hears
the word "Niagara Falls," because that's where his wife, on
their honeymoon, cheated on him). Gleason would say,
"We did that last week," whereupon the wheel comic might
answer with some genteel expression like "Go fuck yourself."

Sometimes, Jackie might get more laughs than the others thought he should. When this happened, the other comics would bring the chorus out behind the curtain and
rehearse new tap routines. The tapping would drown out
Jackie's punch lines. When the audience couldn't hear the
jokes, the men would start yelling for Ada Leonard or
Hinda Wassau or one of the other strippers.

"I fought those road comics every show but I never
buckled down to them. If I had, I'd probably be driving a
bus in Newark today. Breaking up the tap dancer or juggler
became a way of life with me. I knew then that if I could
get laughs under those conditions at the Empire, I could
get laughs anywhere."

□

By the middle of 1936, burlesque was making Jackie more and more popular in northern New Jersey. A Jersey City radio station gave him an hour's program called "Gleason's Madhouse." He also wrote a joke column for the *Jersey Observer*. Neither job paid much money, but it spread the Gleason name and the Gleason comedy.

Jackie met a young friend about this time, a skinny guy who worked part-time as a copy boy for a newspaper and sang for nothing on radio and in dinky clubs, just to be heard. Jackie and Frank Sinatra became lifelong friends from this early meeting.

While Gleason was working these two jobs in 1936, he shared a room with a singing waiter named Tony Amico, who also worked at the Club Miami. They paid three bucks apiece for a single room in a place called Mother Mutzenbacher's. Both aspired to move up the street to a fancier place called Schary's Manor, run by Mama Schary and her son Isadore, who was always writing.

(Years later, Jackie would meet the son in Hollywood, where he had shortened his name to Dore Schary and was running MGM studios, biggest in town.

"He never gave me a job," Jackie remembers.)

Gleason was coming up in the world. When he first started with Sammy Birch, it was three to a room. In Newark, it was two. Jackie and Tony used to argue every night about who was going to get out of bed and turn out the single bulb that illuminated the room. (Tony later worked for Jackie when he made it big in television.)

One night, they had a violent argument over whose turn it was. Jackie, who was reading a Manhattan newspaper, set fire to it and threw it in a wastebasket. It caught the wallpaper on fire. Mother Mutzenbacher tossed them out on their derrieres. Fortunately, Tony owned a car and they slept in that for a few nights. Mother finally took them back because the two were always good for a few laughs—and sometimes the rent.

Club regular Tony Zoppi remembers Jackie as a comedian who even did a trumpet solo.

"I thought he was another Louis Armstrong," Zoppi recalls. "Then years later, a musician told me that Gleason only fingered the trumpet. The bandleader was blowing it behind the curtain."

Jackie, still using Berle's material, also did Milton's schtick of getting into every act. One night Jackie, fortified with Scotch, saw that the Italian husband-and-wife knife-throwing act was dying onstage to a chorus of boos. They had had an argument right before the show. Gleason calmly walked onstage and gently pushed the wife away from the board and leaned against it himself. He got heavy applause, because it was a gutsy thing to do.

"Fortunately, La Rosa was too much of a pro to let his temper get the best of him. He grazed my face a couple of times when he threw those knives, but in fairness, the guy never drew any blood. I can't think of anything I ever did in show business that got more applause than that knife-throwing bit. I never did it again, however."

Columnists all over New Jersey took a great liking to Jackie because he was always good for a funny line. He drank with all, and usually he had a beautiful doll on his arm. He was also popular with other comics in the area because when one of them opened, Jackie always showed up onstage with him to help him get started.

Jackie also was big at benefits, especially for the police. He never turned down the cops. Once the Police Benevolent League of Newark threw a tremendous benefit to help crippled kids. It was such a big affair that only big-name comics like Berle and Youngman were imported from New York. This upset George Sossin, the Club Miami owner, no end. He argued with the police commissioner that if Gleason was good enough for all their other benefits, he was good enough for this one, too. The commissioner okayed Jackie for a twenty-minute opening act.

Jackie started off doing his regular Club Miami act. His fans yelled and screamed, and those who had never seen him before joined in, screaming just as loud. He was on a roll and he knew it. After about half an hour of solid yaks from the audience, he asked the bandleader to play "A Pretty Girl Is Like a Melody." Jackie then did a comic takeoff on Hinda Wassau, the famous stripper of that era. He did all the bumps and grinds, even throwing it up into the balcony and taking the curtain between his legs in the classic stripper tradition. It was a smashing finale, and he walked offstage to heavy applause.

While he was waiting to go out for his bow, Henrietta, George's girlfriend, handed him a typewritten piece of paper. Gleason glanced at it and memorized it in the few seconds he was offstage. Then, for an encore, he went out and did what he had just read. It was Berle's opening monologue, and Jackie doesn't know until this day how Henrietta got a hold of it. Everybody thought it was the funniest monologue they had ever heard—except for Berle, who was fuming so much that he refused to go on. Jackie had to pad time, so he did Youngman's routine. This didn't faze Youngman, even though he also heard it. Henny, who has made a comeback every thirty seconds of his life onstage, went on and did the same one-liners.

Jackie thus turned the benefit for which he had originally been overlooked into a personal tour de force. It would keep him at the Club Miami, off and on, for the next three years. He worked other clubs, mostly joints, around northern New Jersey, sometimes even making Philadelphia.

He had his choice of chorus girls and burlesque queens and always plenty of booze. But Genevieve Halford was

□

always on his mind. He dated her as often as he could find time. There was one problem, though: Every time they went out, Genevieve talked only marriage. They were both twenty years old, which Jackie felt was a little young to settle down. Jackie was making good money, more than most young married couples had at that time, but much as he loved Gen, he knew that they were an original odd couple. She was as good as he was bad.

Gen, too, was still in show business, dancing in the chorus of a club in Yorkville, the German section in the Upper East Side of Manhattan. She saved every cent she made. Jackie spent every penny he made—and then some. It was not a situation conducive to harmony in those Depression years. But Genevieve wanted marriage, and she gave Jackie an ultimatum: either he came around, or she would go out with other guys.

One night Jackie went onstage at the Club Miami, and sitting ringside was Gen with a handsome aviator. In those days, no one was considered more dashing than a pilot. Women swooned over Clark Gable, who often played rakish pilots in the movies. Jackie couldn't keep his eyes off those two at ringside. Why she picked the Club Miami for her first non-Gleason date is something all women will easily comprehend. Jackie didn't like the way the guy was looking at Genevieve.

"I don't blame him. She was one gorgeous dish back then," says Jackie. At the end of his act, he sat down with the two, and Gen introduced him to her date. Gleason had barely acknowledged the introduction when, Ralph-Kramden-like, he blurted out to Genevieve, "Okay, Gen. You got it."

"Got what?" asked Gen.

"Marriage, that's what," shouted Jackie.

It was not the most romantic proposal ever made, but Jackie Gleason, the Brooklyn sharpie, had just fallen for one of woman's oldest ploys.

□

41

·5·
JACKIE GLEASON, HUSBAND

After that marriage proposal, Jackie found himself nervous onstage, something unusual for him. Ever impulsive, Jackie now wanted to get married immediately, just as he always wanted food and drink immediately. He was sure that the handsome aviator was on the make for the girl he loved.

Jackie, who had not yet received an answer to his unorthodox proposal, knew that he had to move fast. A few nights later, he and Sossin, after the Club Miami midnight show, took a cab and made the long jump from Newark to Yorkville. Gen was dancing in the chorus when they got there for the 2 A.M. show at the Half Moon Café. A young tenor was singing with a lone spotlight on him. The chorus danced softly behind him and Jackie remembers that Gen

□

looked especially beautiful in the dim light. After the show ended, she joined Jackie and George at their table.

Jackie started to scream out another marriage proposal but Gen interrupted him. She asked Jackie if he had had masses said for his mother; if he had been to confession lately or to holy communion. Jackie thought he was in church instead of a nightclub, and again he started screaming, perfecting Ralph Kramden then and there. "I can't wait any longer, Gen. I want to get married right now. Tonight."

All the other late-hour patrons were staring at him as Gen kept trying to soften his yelling. Finally, he quieted when Gen said she would come down to Newark that afternoon. Then he started screaming again. He didn't want her working in this joint. Joint? Compared to the Club Miami, it was the Persian Room of the Plaza.

She did come down to Newark that early September day in 1936, and this time accepted a new screaming proposal from Jackie. Even though he was Jewish, George Sossin took over all of the wedding plans for the Catholic ceremony. He knew a priest; Jackie did not. George got a diamond wedding ring from a fence he knew for sixty bucks, and it was George who set up the nuptial mass in St. Columba's Church in Newark.

Tony Amico, the best man, rented a tuxedo, but Jackie had one from his act. Gen's beautiful sister Geraldine was maid of honor. Everybody from the club showed up, except the chef, who was miffed because just the night before, Jackie had ad-libbed onstage that the chef's gravy was now being bottled and sold as wallpaper paste. Cousin Renée represented Jackie's family, and she recalls:

"It was grand and Gen was a vision. It was the kind of Catholic wedding that Gen wanted. It couldn't have been prettier. The one thing I remember about it is that Jackie, at the reception, didn't take a drink. Imagine that, an Irishman not drinking at his own wedding? Not even a champagne toast."

Sossin, who had arranged everything, also tossed the reception at the Club Miami. It was first cabin all the way, and as Jackie recalls, the food must have been catered by Luchow's. It was not the same fare the regular customers ate. A sober Jackie got up and did his act. That's what abstinence does to an Irish comedian.

By this time, Jackie was making sixty-four dollars a week at the Club Miami. At the reception, Gen got another ten out of the champagne-sodden George. Seventy-four dollars a week, plus the fifty that the Empire Burlesque was now paying him, made Jackie a prosperous comedian for those days. And he was only twenty years old.

There was no honeymoon because Jackie had two club shows to do that night; the burlesque house had given him a day off to get married. Tony moved out of the room at Mother Mutzenbacher's and Gen moved in. Mother Mutzenbacher's wasn't exactly Bermuda, and Newark was no Waikiki Beach but, hell, a honeymoon is great anyplace.

Gen was a virginal bride and Jackie was a loving and gentle husband. September 20, 1936, was a great day in Newark for a happy couple of newlyweds.

It was the end of Gen's dancing career at the Half Moon Café in Yorkville; too far to commute from Newark. But she talked Sossin into adding a chorus line in the Club Miami, with George's girlfriend Henrietta and two other chorines. The girls formed a backdrop to Jackie's act. Gen also was choreographer and costume designer. Total income in the Gleason household now was a little better than a hundred and fifty bucks a week.

As the marriage moved into 1937, a hundred and fifty

□

bucks wasn't enough for the Gleason life-style. They moved into a small apartment, but try as she did, Gen could not break Jackie of his pick-up-the-check spending habits. He could spend money much faster than Gen could save it. One February day in 1937, finances were so tough that Jackie got hold of a bunch of brochures from a local furniture store advertising a one-cent sale. Each brochure had a penny pasted on it, and Jackie tore them all off to buy a couple of sandwiches for the two of them.

There was only one thing to do. Much as he hated to, Jackie had to leave the Club Miami. George was a good friend, but being a good friend, he understood that it was time for Jackie to step up in class. Gleason's next move didn't advance him that much financially—the pay was about the same—but it was a high-class club, not a "joint" like the Club Miami. His next job was at Frank Donato's Colonial Inn in Singac, New Jersey.

Donato, like Sossin, was sold on Jackie's potential as a comedian. He even got Jackie a manager—by the name of Willie Webber. Willie only handled comedians, and as soon as he caught Gleason's act, he signed him. Donato also tried to get his *paisano* friend, Sinatra, to be a client of Webber's. Frank was a production singer at the Colonial, working for little or nothing.

"Sorry," said Webber, "I don't handle singers," thus making what could roughly be called a fifty-million-dollar mistake.

Gleason was a big hit at the Colonial, even bigger than he had been at the Club Miami, and he soon attracted talent scouts. One night Gleason saw a short, bald-headed guy sitting ringside with a face only Charlie Chaplin could love. Immediatley, Jackie saw him as a great stooge for his act. The almost-stooge was George ("Bullets") Durgom, today a legendary manager of Hollywood talent. Bullets was then road manager for Tommy Dorsey's orchestra, and he was at the Colonial looking at singer Connie Haines for Dorsey's Pied Pipers. Bullets was not interested in becoming Gleason's stooge.

"Little did I know that night," Jackie recalls, "that both my pal Sinatra and Connie would wind up with Tommy Dorsey, and that that little bald-headed guy [Durgom] would someday become my manager and get me a fabulous eleven-million-dollar deal with CBS-TV, biggest deal ever in television at that time [1952]."

Jackie worked for some months at the Colonial Club, attracting a lot of his old friends from nearby Newark and making a lot of new ones who wouldn't have been caught dead in the Club Miami. Most of the customers who came to the Colonial were big spenders who came with their girlfriends—seldom their wives. All of them, Jackie especially, liked to party after hours. Like most nightclub performers, Jackie liked to unwind with the guys he got wound up with in the first place. Singac was a great hideaway spot and Gleason was the local celebrity. So when the columnists saw all this horseplay with the "broads" after hours, it was Jackie's name that got in the columns. Naturally, Gen would read these items. If she missed one, there was always the well-intentioned friend who called it to her attention. It was hard for Jackie to explain when he came home each dawn.

"Gen became very concerned about my behavior. She just couldn't understand why I had to unwind with this crowd, instead of coming home to her."

Jackie invited her to come along with him, but she didn't want to. And to tell the truth, Jackie really didn't want her out in that after-hours crowd, where every guy was trying to get laid. Jackie swears he didn't mess with any of the girls himself, but try to get a wife waiting up for you at sunrise to believe that.

"Gen was too nice, too religious. She was—and is—one of the nicest girls you will ever meet. I would have made a good hoodlum, and that is why she was attracted to me in the first place. Nice girls are always attracted to guys like me. It's that motherly reform instinct. After a while, that hoodlumism is not so damn attractive to a wife. Gen wanted me home. I didn't come home. And she couldn't cope with it. I don't blame her one damn bit."

Gen came from show business herself, but she was totally unlike the typical showgirls and chorines. She was an accomplished dancer, a ballerina. The people Jackie thought of as friends Gen considered bums. For the most part, she was right, with one notable exception. Gen, we all know, was Mother Cabrini in leotards, so she urged Jackie to take his marital problems to Bishop Fulton J. Sheen, then the golden voice of radio, who was without doubt the greatest pulpit orator of that time.

Well, Bishop Sheen and Jackie took to each other like long-lost pals. They became the best of friends, and Jackie spent hours—sometimes entire nights—in the Bishop's Manhattan apartment arguing about religion and theology.

What had started out as a happy marriage now became a bickering, miserable one. It was mostly Jackie's fault, and he admits it. All Gen wanted was a normal husband who came home from work like other men do. Jackie wasn't a normal husband.

They stuck together through 1937 and 1938, but there was no way he'd quit unwinding with the boys—and often the showgirls—after work. Jackie was always threatening to leave, and Gen was always threatening to kick him out. But they stuck together, mostly because of their Catholicism. And they still loved each other, which made it all the worse. (Cousin Renée still keeps in touch with Gen, and says that Gen still loves Jackie.)

Jackie left the Colonial Club and worked all over New Jersey. He would play Cranberry Lake, Asbury Park, anyplace with water nearby, in the summertime. In the winter, he would play the Rathskeller in Philadelphia or go back to the Colonial. This pattern went on for three years. Once when he heard his old friend George Sossin was having it rough at the Club Miami, Jackie took a cut in pay to help him out. No emcee since had been as popular as Jackie was in the old days. The Club Miami, however, was not long for this world, and it eventually folded.

In between nightclub jobs, Jackie would again emcee auto thrill shows. He had learned early how to get laughs with cars getting smashed all around him, but his free spending at the bar was still haunting his marriage. Things got so bad financially that, in 1939, Gen moved in with her folks in Jackson Heights, Queens, to save money, while Jackie took a job at the Wannamassa Gardens in Asbury Park, moving into a small boardinghouse along the Atlantic Ocean.

Jackie's bar bill at the Wannamassa soon outdistanced his rent payments, and he got way in hock. He pulled the old trick of throwing his suitcase out of the window into some bushes. Then, in bathrobe and trunks, he casually strolled through the lobby, towel on shoulder, and was ostensibly bound for the beach. Instead, he rounded the corner, got his suitcase out of the bushes, changed his clothes and vanished. He stiffed the rent but, true to form, he came back three years later to pay the landlady back.

"To hell with the rent," she screamed. "You're alive! We all thought you had drowned!"

Meanwhile, the arguments over his life of sin, the all-night parties with the girls and the booze, all made for an unhappy home life—when he did come home. Gen couldn't understand how he could cavort with girls who undressed for a living and remain pure himself, and she was right.

For the most part, Jackie confined his all-night carousing to booze, but occasionally, he would jump on a shapely chorus girl.

"Unfortunately, I was honest with Gen and told her about these one-night affairs. In retrospect, I should have kept my mouth shut. They meant nothing to me, and I told her, she was the only one I loved. It's much better to be discreet about one's peccadilloes."

It really was an odd marriage. Jackie not only loved Gen, he worshipped her. Gen, devout as she was, would have loved to share more of Jackie's life. Most wives would have kicked a husband like Jackie out years before she did. Gen held on, however, and on July 31, 1939, when Jackie was twenty-three years old, daughter Geraldine was born. She was named after Gen's sister, the other half of the Halford Twins ballerina act. Cousin Renée recalls:

"That baby did something to Jackie, something that Gen had never been able to do. He came home after his show so he could play with his daughter at the two A.M. feeding."

But it didn't last all that long. He soon went back to his old ways, making early-morning dates with leggy strippers and showgirls. And, as always, there was the all-night drinking. Sometimes, Gen would hear of his transgressions. More often, busy with a new baby, she would not. Still, when a husband comes home at dawn drunk, a wife knows he didn't spend the night in an all-night library.

Newark and most of northern New Jersey is no farther away from Manhattan than Queens, but in terms of Jackie's career, the Hudson River might just as well have been the Rocky Mountains. The East River, inexplicably, did not pose that great a barrier. Willie Webber, knowing all this, got Jackie a booking in the Queen's Terrace in 1940. Willie knew that he could get a Manhattan club owner out to Queens to see his boy. New Jersey was another planet.

Webber had realized what a great comedian Jackie could be, that he just needed the proper showcase, the proper control and direction. Willie had a long-range plan. He wanted Jackie in the Club 18, then the "in" club for the Broadway crowd. The Fifty-second Street club attracted all of show business, both Broadway and Hollywood. It also was the hangout for all the famous columnists, who wielded incredible power over a young performer's career: Walter Winchell, Ed Sullivan, Leonard Lyons, Louis Sobol, Damon Runyon, sportswriter Jimmy Cannon, Bob Considine, and later, Earl Wilson and Jack O'Brian.

Most managers would rather have seen their clients unemployed than tossed into the Club 18 arena, home of the ad-lib insult and controlled lunacy. But Webber knew this kind of club would be Jackie's meat. All Willie had to do was to hustle Fred Lamb, one of the Club 18's owners, out to the Queen's Terrace to catch Jackie's act.

Jackie didn't know that Lamb was in the audience. It probably would have made no difference. One thing Gleason always had in abundant supply was self-confidence.

Now, Fred Lamb *never* laughed. He was laughed out after listening to comics for years and years; he had heard every joke. When he caught Jackie, he gave him his supreme accolade. He said the single word—"Funnee."

It would be the most important move in Gleason's career when Lamb decided Jackie was ready to be thrown

□

among the Club 18's den of lions. In Pat Harrington, Sr., Frankie Hyers and Jack White, the Club 18 had three of the zaniest comics ever to hit Broadway. They were out- rageous, mad, crazy and totally unpredictable. They would have destroyed the Marx Brothers on a good night.

It was Gleason's kind of show.

▪ 6 ▪
THE
BIG
BREAK

In the days before Pearl Harbor, in 1940 and 1941, Fifty-second Street was the hub of Manhattan's nightclub business. It was "Swing Street," and jazz greats like Louis Prima and Wingy Manone had their own clubs. On some nights, the musicians outnumbered the customers, but it made no difference; jazz was the musicians' own entertainment. If the customers liked it, so much gravy.

All of the legendary starmakers worked the street, the agents who could get you on tomorrow's 20th Century Limited or Super Chief headed for the Coast, as Hollywood was known in those days—Irving ("Swifty") Lazar, Sonny Werblin and the fledgling Lew Wasserman were but a few. The legendary Toots Shor was a bruiser of a bouncer at

Leon and Eddie's, years before he would own the most famous saloon in New York on the very same spot.

It was a street frequented by gangsters and would-be gangsters—who often were worse—such as Louis ("Pretty") Amberg, who once punched Louis Prima in his Famous Door club because Louis refused to play a tune Pretty requested. (Pretty got his name because he had a face that looked like thirty miles of dirt road. He was noted for slapping showgirls in public. He later was fried to death in his own car after one of his enemies had chopped him up a bit with an axe.)

Most of the clubs were dedicated to jazz, sometimes striptease, but it was the comics who made the street. Gone are such clubs as the Royal Box, the Moulin Rouge, the Onyx, the Three Deuces and, of course, the Club 18, which would be the launching pad for the young Jackie Gleason. Only the chic "21" Club remains, a fancy eatery that began in Prohibition as a speakeasy.

Timing—or luck—plays such an important role in any performer's career, perhaps more so than talent. Not even Willie Webber knew that when Fred Lamb came out to the Queen's Terrace to catch Jackie, he needed a comic for the Club 18 immediately. Just that very afternoon, Pat Harrington, Sr., had informed Lamb that he wanted a leave of absence. He had been moonlighting in a play with Helen Hayes and he wanted to go on national tour with it.

As soon as Lamb saw Gleason perform, he knew he had Harrington's replacement. It was only a few weeks later, in the fall of 1940, that Gleason joined the Club 18 funny farm, but still kept his Queen's Terrace job because the hours didn't conflict. He was making 150 bucks a week with the two jobs and spending $200 a night.

"I'll never forget my first night at the Club 18. I had barely shaken hands with Frankie and Jack when I went on

□

solo. Those bastards wouldn't get onstage with me. They sat facing the stage, with their backs to the audience and dared me to be funny. Then they started heckling me.

"I loved it. This was my dish. I tore them to shreds; I insulted everybody in the club—the owners, the celebrities, the columnists. Frankie and Jack started to slink out. I yelled, 'Come back, you cowards, and watch The Great One work.' I think that was the first time I ever used that expression and I'm still using it."

Whenever they came to New York, all the Hollywood crowd met at the Club 18—Jimmy Cagney, John Garfield, Pat O'Brien, Clark Gable, Robert Taylor, Carole Lombard, Frank Morgan, Spencer Tracy, Humphrey Bogart, Gary Cooper, Errol Flynn, you name them. And stars of the Broadway hit shows—Bert Lahr, Louis Calhern, Willie and Eugene Howard, Milton Berle, Ethel Merman, Victor Moore, Mae West—all were regulars. Jimmy Cannon, one of the all-time great sportswriters, was a nightly customer. Occasionally, the great Joe Frisco, most quoted comic and hoofer on Broadway, would join the Club 18 troupe. When he did, the other comics did a Good-Time Charlie routine with him. Good-Time Charlie was a visiting butter-and-egg man from the Farm Belt who came to the big city with lots of money, looking for broads. Frisco made his entrance through the front door on the cue "Here comes Good-Time Charlie now." What followed was ad-lib humor at its finest, because no one ever had the fast quips Frisco did, even though he stuttered.

One night, while waiting for his cue. Frisco went across the street to the "21" Club to have a few drinks. The city had torn up Fifty-second Street at this time and the street was filled with excavations. Frisco, sober, had maneuvered his way around the trenches going over to Club

"21," but coming back, after a few stiff belts, was another matter entirely.

Gleason gave the cue: "Here comes Good-Time Charlie now." No Frisco. He gave it three more times and then decided to see what the hell had happened to Joe. Jackie heard a faint cry of help from deep down in one of the city's trenches. He knew it was Joe right away because it took almost a full minute for the single word "Help" to come out.

When Jackie pulled him out, Joe said, "I-I-I am w-w-w-walking across the damn s-street and all of a sudden, I-I-I am back in W-W-W-World W-W-W-War One."

For the next few months, Jackie was a big hit at the Club 18 with his fresh brand of insult humor, predating Jack E. Leonard and Don Rickles. He didn't care whom he insulted, the bigger the name, the worse the insult. And one night, early in 1941, a distinguished-looking tycoon came into the Club 18 and Gleason really let him have it, although he had no idea whom he was insulting.

The guy's hairline was receding, so Gleason said, "Is that your head, sir? Or are you diapering a baby?"

Everybody who knew the tycoon looked to see how he was taking these insults. All knew that if one of his three thousand employees ever kidded him about his coming baldness, it would have meant an instant pink slip. But the guy was rolling over with laughter, because Jack L. Warner, one of the biggest studio bosses in Hollywood history, was a frustrated comic himself.

Jack would sooner tell a lousy joke than make a good picture, and he often did both. He was worth $100 million dollars but he would gladly have given half of it to be Henny Youngman.

For example, once Jack entertained Madame Chiang Kai-shek at a studio luncheon. Since her husband the Generalissimo was running the vast country at the time, she came with a huge entourage of Chinese functionaries. Warner looked over this group and this was his opening line: "Seeing this distinguished group reminds me that I forgot to send out my laundry today." There was some laughter but it was all hysterical, mostly from studio employees.

Another time, at the first day's shooting of *Giant,* Elizabeth Taylor, the star, asked me to go with her to a welcoming luncheon. She had never worked on the Warner lot before. Jack came to our table and asked me to introduce him to the beautiful young star. Elizabeth flashed her lavender eyes and expected the usual flowery speech of welcome. Instead, she heard this from Warner: "Most people like a moon to make love. I'll take a double bed."

All of this explains why Jack L. Warner did what he did at the Club 18 on that night in 1941. Gleason did not know whom he had insulted, and he took off jauntily for his other show at the Queen's Terrace. When he came back, Willie Webber, Fred Lamb, Hyers and White all chorused that he had a contract to go to Hollywood, a $250-a-week contract at Warner Bros.

No one before—or since—has ever made Hollywood by insulting a studio boss.

Jackie's arrival in Hollywood was uneventful because Jack Warner, with typical Hollywood indifference, never told anyone why he had signed Gleason—or even what he was. Jackie even had trouble getting in the studio gate that first day—the cop on the gate had to make a call to the personnel department first.

Fortunately, he didn't have to wait long before he got cast in a movie called *Navy Blues,* in which he played a sailor. The stars of the movie were three other Jacks— Oakie, Haley and Carson. All were big Hollywood names

(Jack Haley was the Tin Man in *The Wizard of Oz*), and they could have kissed Gleason off as just another bit contract player. Instead, they all became his mentors and lifelong friends.

When the movie was previewed at Warners' Hollywood Theater, Gleason was the only one of the four Jacks who attended. He called up the other three and told them, "I looked like I was standing on a corner in a sailor suit watching a movie being made."

Jackie got hooked up with another hard-drinking pal in *All Through the Night,* in which he played a gangster. The pal, who was star of the 1942 movie, was Humphrey Bogart. In *Larceny Inc.* he got cast with another gangster, Edward G. Robinson, but this time Eddie played a Runyonesque type of gangster, not "Little Caesar."

Warners loaned him out to 20th Century–Fox to play Betty Grable's manager in *Springtime in the Rockies.* About the closest he ever came to comedy in that early movie career was when he co-starred with comedian Jack Durant in something called *Tramp, Tramp, Tramp.* No one around town even remembers the title, let alone the movie. Another loan-out to Fox cast him as a bass fiddle player in the Glenn Miller band in a picture called *Orchestra Wives.*

Bullets Durgom recalls that the only laughs in this picture came off camera because Gleason was the only person alive who could make Miller laugh. Glenn had some kind of side pain that only surfaced when he laughed; hence, he never laughed—until Gleason came along and had Miller rolling in laughter and pain.

Hollywood didn't know exactly what to do with Gleason, who didn't fit the Hollywood mode of a funny man. He was too handsome, for one thing. In those early Hollywood years, Jackie looked like a heavy Robert Taylor, then the screen's reigning handsome hero. Director Archie Mayo at Warners told Gleason to shed some weight, and he would make him a leading man. Jackie, in a terrible ordeal, got rid of fifty pounds. Mayo then told him he was too thin—and not funny anymore. You have to be around Hollywood for years to understand how this could happen. It's how the town has always operated. Hollywood is not a town, it's a Gilbert and Sullivan operetta.

Oakie, his mentor, helped Jackie perfect all those moves that later were to prove so hilarious on television. Oakie, who could drink a bottle of Scotch in ninety minutes and did so almost nightly, introduced Jackie to all the town's hot spots. Haley, a moderate drinker, drove the two Jacks home when they needed it, also almost nightly.

Flo Haley, widow of Jack Haley, recalls: "The first thing I noticed about Jackie Gleason when he first came to Hollywood was that he always picked up the check. No one could pay if Gleason was drinking with you. And it used to burn up my Jack that some of the Hollywood crowd, many of them making much more money than Jackie, would let the check ride until Gleason showed up. It was criminal how some of the Hollywood phonies sponged off Gleason."

Jackie didn't bring Gen and the children—daughter Linda, born September 16, was too tiny to make the trip in the fall of 1941—out to Hollywood with him. He often was seen in the company of shapely starlets, of which Hollywood always has an ample supply. They got his name in the gossip columns, but surprisingly, one encounter that Louella Parsons and Hedda Hopper missed was with a superstar.

Jackie found himself on a radio show with Joan Crawford, also a world-class drinker. "I have heard a lot about you," said Joan to the handsome Jackie.

"And I've heard a lot about you," said Jackie, and he wasn't kidding.

□

After the show, Joan invited Jackie to stop by her place for a drink. Jackie recalls that she served 100 proof booze that would have knocked off W. C. Fields' head. Joan, who put cleanliness above godliness, made Jackie take off his shoes before he walked on her white carpets. It seemed incongruous to him at the time, because Joan had about six poodles, who were pooping all over the rugs.

"Better you should give your guests boots, Joan, instead of making them take off their shoes," said Jackie. He remembers that his comment got no laugh from the meticulous Joan.

Jackie and Joan sat down on a couch, also white, while she mixed several rounds of drinks. Before long, the comic and star were feeling no pain. She snuggled closer to Jackie, who sensed what was coming. He said, "You don't mean to tell me I am going to kiss Joan Crawford?"

She said, "Well, you are, right now."

After they had kissed, he grabbed his shoes and beat it for the door. There, he turned around and said, "It's been a great night for Brooklyn."

Jackie saw Jack Warner only once during his year's contract at Warners. Warner was driving in the gate one day in 1942 just as Jackie was walking out. Warner hit Jackie with some of the same lines Gleason had used on him on that memorable night at the Club 18 the year before.

No one knew better than Gleason that, despite Warner's remembering him, he was lost in the shuffle at the studio. They didn't know what in the hell to do with him, a common plaint among many contract players of the studio system. When his year was about up, he auditioned over at Universal for the Goldstein twins—Bob and Leonard. They were big producers on the Universal lot, and Jackie remembers how impressed he was with Bob, who was having his toenails cut during the audition for some long-forgotten comedy. The twins gave Jackie the same story he had heard too many times before—he was too good-looking to be funny. (Just look at pictures of Gleason from those early days.)

His pals, Oakie and Haley, advised him to take the money—$250 a week—and run. Run he did, to the nearest bar. Besides Oakie, he now had three other hard-drinking cronies—Martha Raye, comedian Sid Silvers and the burlesque comedian Rags Ragland, who had a contract at MGM.

When Jackie didn't make it as a movie star, he blamed it partly on his lack of acting experience. After all, his only stage experience was in a play called *Keep Off the Grass,* a part he had gotten after his first two months at the Club 18 in 1940. The only good thing about that forgettable show was its cast—Jimmy Durante, Jane Froman, Ray Bolger, Virginia O'Brien, and Gleason. Virginia, the deadpan singer of so many MGM musicals, recalls it played longer on its Boston tryout (four weeks) then it did on Broadway (three weeks).

Except for his lasting friendship with Jack Oakie and Jack Haley, the only good thing about that first Hollywood visit was Slapsy Maxie's, the famous Hollywood nightclub. Jackie loved working there as much as he did at the Club 18. Sammy Lewis owned the club, but it was named after Maxie Rosenbloom, light-heavyweight champion of the world from 1930 to 1934. Maxie got his nickname from his slapping punch, but also because he had been slapped back a little too often in the head.

Gleason and Rosenbloom, now an entertainer, often clashed both onstage and off. Jackie was an ad-libber; Maxie had to work from cues in the script. One night Jackie ad-libbed a line about Maxie's battered face, which

looked like a topographical map of the Himalayas.
"I know I'm ugly. I had four hundred fights. What's
your excuse?" Maxie shot back in a surprising ad-lib.
"I bet on you," said Gleason. At that, Maxie chased
Jackie offstage and up and down the aisles, bent on may-
hem.

Gleason and Maxie shared a hotel suite for a while,
which inspired a couple of Gleason's more famous practical
jokes. One night, Maxie got drunk and showed up in the
suite with a ten-dollar hooker. He passed out cold and the
hooker left, fortunately having gotten her ten dollars in advance. Gleason hurried down to the hotel drugstore and
bought a bottle of Mercurochrome. He then painted the
cock of the sleeping Rosenbloom a vivid red. A few hours
later, Maxie woke up with a bloodcurdling scream. He
showed his flaming-red monster to Gleason, who calmly
told him that the hooker had given him a bad case of Colorado. Now, of course, there is no such disease, but Maxie
was on the phone to his doctor, explaining for half an hour
that he had a bad case of Colorado. The doctor didn't
know what in the hell he was talking about.

Another time, Jackie laced one of Maxie's supposito-
ries with Tabasco sauce; he knew that the champ had a bad
case of hemorrhoids. That bloodcurdling scream was even
worse than the first.

Jackie had a friendly little feud going with Sammy
Lewis, the owner. No nightclub owner wants to see his star
comic drinking all the time, and Sammy put the flag up on
Gleason at the club. No problem—Jackie just went across
the street to another bar between shows. In desperation, in
the summer of 1942, Sammy had Gleason move into his
house, where he could keep a better eye on him. Sammy
never left the house without first locking up his liquor cabinet. Jackie would invite girls in for a party and Sammy

□

would come home later to find all his liquor gone, but with the lock untouched on the cabinet. It became a big mystery, almost driving Sammy to the funny farm.

It was months before Sammy figured out that Gleason had taken a screwdriver—the hardware kind—and removed the back of the cabinet. Then, when the liquor was gone, he screwed the back on again.

One of Jackie's final shows at Slapsy Maxie's is still remembered by many in Hollywood as a comedy classic. He came onstage one night to find Robert Taylor sitting ringside. Just by coincidence that afternoon back in 1942, Jackie had seen Taylor's big picture *Johnny Eager.* Jackie did his own two hour ad-libbed version of the movie, playing Taylor, Lana Turner and Van Heflin. Everybody in the place was rolling on the floor except Sammy. Gleason, in Sammy's opinion, was on too damn long, and he wasn't doing his regular act.

But despite all his new drinking buddies and the always available party girls, Jackie missed Gen and his young daughters, and a few days after that famous show, he was on a Ford Trimotor flying back home to his family and Broadway. At Phoenix, Arizona, the plane developed engine trouble and made an emergency landing. Jackie was in no mood to wait for another plane, so he decided to make the rest of the trip by train—except he didn't have enough money.

Gleason the con man went to work when he found no bank would cash an out-of-state check. He convinced a local merchant to cash it by first taking him to see *Navy Blues,* which happened to be playing at a nearby movie house. When Jackie first appeared on the screen, the merchant was convinced that Jackie indeed was who he said he was, but he liked the picture, so Jackie had to sit through the whole show before he got his check cashed.

□

Back in New York, Gen took him in but only for a few months. She had read of his capers in Hollywood, and he was soon back to his old tricks in New York. There was a lot of bickering. Jackie said, "We can't go on fighting like this in front of the children." The girls, both toddlers, may have been too young to notice the bickering, but Jackie moved out anyway. He moved into the Hotel Hudson, but not for long; he got evicted for the particularly annoying habit of staging parties after midnight with Max Kaminsky's Dixieland Ragpickers band.

Willie Webber got Jackie a job in the Rathskeller in Philadelphia, but the third night there, he fell down a flight of steps and broke his arm. A doctor set it and told Jackie to come back the next day, that it needed a more thorough resetting. Instead, Jackie threw an all-night party to celebrate the broken arm and never went back to the doctor.

Jackie next went back to the Club 18 at a whopping six hundred bucks a week, four times what he had earned when he first went there three years earlier in 1940. Jack White, now running the club, was aghast when Jackie showed up with his huge camel's hair polo coat draped over a broken arm, still in a cast. Jackie did about twenty minutes of broken-arm jokes that soothed Jack somewhat, but probably not six hundred dollars' worth.

This was all happening in 1943, in the middle of World War II, and Jackie, as a father, was classified 3-A. But then draft boards began calling up fathers. (Much publicity was given to Erastus Corning, the mayor of Albany, who had eleven children and was drafted.) Jackie was called up. He was made 4-F for a variety of reasons: excessive weight, a right arm that hadn't healed properly, some numbness in his fingers and a few minor complaints. (Being 4-F meant that he would be called to service only when Adolf Hitler marched into Toots Shor's and asked for some schnapps.)

□

In January of 1943, Jackie pulled something off that anyone who remembers New York in those days, when the only way to get a hotel room was to bribe the manager, will find impossible to believe. A natural con man, he talked Robert Christenberry, a fan from the Club 18, into giving corner suites at the Hotel Astor to both Jackie and Jay C. Flippen, an actor-vaudevillian and drinking buddy of Jackie's, at no charge whatsoever. Furthermore, they could sign for food, booze and laundry. By way of contrast, Jimmy Durante, a much bigger star, had only a tiny room on the same floor of the Times Square hotel, and Durante had to pay for everything.

Jackie remembers that it was impossible to get whiskey in bottles during the war, so he had room service send up his booze in pitchers. No great inconvenience. "We threw lots of parties and always invited our pal Durante. We felt sorry for him paying for everything in that small room."

Jackie made one misstep at the Astor. One night, he and Flippen, tired of always staging private parties in their free suites, decided to go out on the town. It was between jobs, so Gleason had no money, and he went to the cashier and asked for a payout of $150. He got it. And Christenberry, when he heard of it, raised holy hell.

"If you ever want money," he told the astonished Gleason, "ask me for it, not the cashier." After that, whenever Gleason and Flippen wanted to go out on the town, they went straight to the manager, who gave them all the cash they needed.

It was inevitable during this time that Jackie would become a drinking buddy of the infamous Toots Shor. Jackie, of course, soon had signing privileges with his pal Toots. Toots had the best bar in New York but his food was terrible. One day in 1943, Jackie called Toots over to his table to complain about a tough piece of steak. "To whom, sir, do I turn in my fountain pen?" he asked Toots.

Frank Sinatra, also 4-F in the draft from a pierced ear-drum, recalls how Gleason would borrow three hundred dollars from Toots, then lay it all on the bar and yell, "Drinks for the house." Frank recalls one night in 1943 when Gleason, with no money, hired a limousine to take himself and Sinatra a few doors down Fifty-second Street to a jazz joint to listen to the one-armed trumpet player, Wingy Manone.

"Gleason borrowed five hundred bucks from Toots to pay for the limousine, which probably cost all of twenty bucks in those days. The rest of the money he kept tossing at Wingy in hundred-dollar bills to play 'That's a Plenty' over and over again.

"When Toots saw that limousine only going less than one hundred feet, he blew his top. He barred both of us from his saloon for a month—but we ignored the ban."

Willie Webber was having a hard sell hustling jobs for Jackie because of his growing reputation as a lover of the sauce. Still, Webber got him a job in a Broadway show called *Along Fifth Avenue,* which didn't last all that long, even with wartime business. He earned six hundred a week, part of which he paid to Christenberry for past favors at the Astor.

Along Fifth Avenue wasn't a great show, but Jackie was great in it. He had the show-stopping scene, a French Foreign Legion sketch that could have been pedestrain with anyone but Gleason. It began with three thirsty legion-naires staggering across the stage before a desert backdrop. It was cliché until Gleason made his entrance. He had re-written the sketch himself, and when he made his entrance he was dressed impeccably in a legionnaire uniform espe-cially tailored for him by Brooks Brothers. In contrast to the bedraggled legionnaires, Gleason looked as if he were

□

in the Fifth Avenue Easter parade. By his side was a shapely blonde in the skimpiest of costumes. She was carrying Gleason's golf bag.

Gleason brushed aside the thirsty legionnaires and then, with a flourish and sweeping arm gesture that he had perfected in burlesque, he said in a Park Avenue tenor, "Do you mind if we play through?"

It took five minutes before the laughter died down in the house. It was one of the great entrances in Broadway history. And for a television audience at least six years away, Jackie Gleason had invented one of his greatest characters—Reggie Van Gleason the Third.

• 7 •
TELEVISION DISCOVERS JACKIE

In between the parties at the Hotel Astor, Jackie would stop by Gen's apartment to see his little girls. Geraldine was four when Jackie was living at the Astor back in 1943; Linda was two. Geraldine recalls:

"I can barely remember Dad showing up at Christmas and other times. It seemed like he would only stay a half-hour or so. Linda and I were too young to know that my mother and father were on the outs. We were always glad to see him. As kids, it was sometimes hard to understand why we didn't see more of him and why our Christmases were not like the other kids had. It bothered us then. It doesn't now. It's just his way of shielding himself. He's not your average father. We know that now. We know he loves us in his own special way and we love him."

☐

It seems as if Jackie hates himself for the way he treated Gen and the kids in those war years. Jackie constantly reiterates that Gen was too damn good for him and never should have married such a wild Irishman.

"I was a hoodlum at heart," Gleason says today—and means it.

When he went out on the town, which was every night, he didn't want Gen along. Her very goodness inhibited his free-swinging style and he thought her far above the Broadway environment. He knew that he was a sucker for every blond showgirl, especially if he had a few drinks in him. The occasions for sin were ever-present in Jackie's life, and he didn't need his arm twisted to take advantage of them.

Willie Webber, meanwhile, had great faith in Jackie as a comedian, so much so that Webber himself thought Jackie needed a manager with more clout. Willie tried to sell Gleason's contract to the Music Corporation of America, then the biggest theatrical talent agency in the business, but his motives weren't all that noble. Willie knew he could make money on the sale and much more in a future split of commissions, and he knew that if Jackie was to make it as a superstar, he needed an MCA contract to do the job.

Jackie wouldn't hear of any sale to MCA. To make sure, he borrowed $150 from Willie and bought him a solid-gold money clip. On it, he had inscribed: "To Willie—the world's best manager . . . Jackie."

Willie got him a booking at Lou Walters' Artists and Models for four hundred dollars a week. (Lou was the father of television's Barbara Walters.) That revue didn't last all that long. Next Jackie worked at Loew's State for $750 per week. He was an emcee, doing the same sort of thing for which he used to get four bucks a night at the Halsey amateur shows in 1934 and 1935.

Toward the end of 1943, Jackie teamed up with comedian Lew Parker in the national company of Olsen and Johnson's hit Broadway musical *Hellzapoppin'*. Teaming Gleason with Parker was like trying to put out fire with gasoline. Lew not only drank like Gleason but he was a compulsive horseplayer as well. Often Jackie never saw his wages from the show. Lew would pick up both checks and leave them at Belmont or Arlington Park.

They did crazy things together. One night in Chicago, Jackie decided he needed a new overcoat. He and Lew went into Marshall Fields and Jackie tried on a coat, but the sleeves were too long. The salesman said he would have them shortened. Jackie said he couldn't wait, grabbed a pair of scissors and cut the sleeves off himself.

Another time, when the show was playing Philadelphia, neither of them knew that Chick Johnson and Ole Olsen were in the audience, checking on the road company. One of the gags had Gleason firing a gun that dropped a flag, reading "Bang." Then a duck dropped down from the ceiling. This night, they got their laugh okay when the duck dropped but the gun didn't go off.

Afterward, Chick Johnson, seriously, asked Gleason and Parker, "Do you know why Olsen and Johnson are big stars?" Before Gleason and Parker could answer, Johnson continued, "Because we always check our guns before each performance."

Gleason delights in telling about Parker's girlfriends. "I don't know how he did it, but every girl he ever got serious about had suicidal tendencies. Lew was always kicking down doors, shutting off gas jets and picking girls off ledges. Finally, he married Betty Kean, who smoked cigars in the Kean Sisters act with sister Jane. I saw him one day and said, 'I bet you're happy now that you got a wife who doesn't want to commit suicide every night.' 'Yeah,' he answered, 'but she leaves cigar butts all over the house.'"

After *Hellzapoppin'* finished its run in 1944, Webber took Jackie along with him to an interview with Sam Rausch, manager of the Roxy, a cathedral of a theater that presented huge stage productions together with first-run movies.

Willie knew that Sam was a Gleason fan from the Club 18 days, and so he asked for the moon—three thousand dollars a week. At this, Gleason let out an awesome scream: "I'm not worth three thousand a week!"

Sam thought this was very funny and okayed the deal, but it was the last time Willie ever took Jackie on an interview. Jackie, who was emcee for the stage show, did only six minutes onstage. When Rausch complained, Jackie told him, "This stuff is so rich, an audience can only take six minutes at a sitting."

Came 1945 and the end of the war, both in Europe and Japan. It was a big year for the Allies, and a big one for Jackie. Willie got him his biggest Broadway break—*Follow the Girls,* with Gertrude Neisen, who ranked with Ethel Merman in the Broadway musical comedy of that era. It was a show mostly about sailors chasing girls and Jackie was a sailor once more, just as in *Navy Blues* at Warners. Only this time, he was damn funny. And at first, he was a little bit too funny for Gertrude.

"I wanted to fire him after opening night," Gertie once said, "but I couldn't after the reviews came in. Everybody is uptight at the beginning of a show and Jackie was ad-libbing too much."

"When someone strays from the script, it's irritating to the other performers, but he got raves from the critics. When I read those, I learned to live with the ad-libs."

□

It was a wild comedy, and Gleason was a big hit working with such a pro as Gertrude. Money was good too—a thousand dollars per week. It almost kept him alive through most of 1945 and 1946. His spending habits, whether broke or rich, were still the same. In 1946, after *Follow the Girls* closed on the road, Jackie's next job paid him $350, quite a comedown. This was the old radio show called "Chamber Music Society of Lower Basin Street," a jazz show that first brought Frank Sinatra and Dinah Shore to a national radio audience.

Gleason got this job through a press agent-friend named Lee Meyers, who was publicizing the music show. He had remembered that Jackie used to play a mean trumpet back in his New Jersey nightclub days. Of course, Meyers didn't know that this part of the act had been a hoax. Jackie had fingered the keys and made like he was blowing the horn, but the actual playing was done behind the curtain by the bandleader.

Lee thought it strange that Jackie refused to rehearse with the orchestra the day of the show. Once again, Jackie conned the band's first trumpet to play behind the curtain, out of sight of the studio audience. Show time came and the two had cooked up a routine. After a few blasts on the trumpet, Jackie would drop the horn and ad-lib a few musician jokes. He wanted to keep the show musical.

The producer immediately saw that the trumpet playing was a hoax, and he was about ready to fire Meyers and Gleason both when he noticed a strange thing. The audience was laughing, which was not all that unusual, but so were the musicians—now that's unusual. (Musicians, as a rule, are the worst laughers in show business.)

After the show, the station's switchboard lit up. All the callers said it was the funniest show they had ever heard. Gleason was such a hit that the show started using

□

comedians, preferably those with musical talent. Victor Borge, the funny Danish concert pianist, got his start on that show and soon became a fixture on the Rudy Vallee Fleischman Hour, one of the top radio shows of the post-war era.

From the radio show, Willie booked Jackie into clubs all over the place—the Northwood Inn in suburban Detroit, back at the Rathskeller in Philadelphia and the prestigious Capitol in the Times Square theatrical district. This was the same house where Bob Hope had been playing when Jackie first landed in Manhattan with thirty-one cents in his pocket. This time, Jimmy Dorsey and his band were the headline attraction, and Gleason was booked as special guest star.

Gleason's contract read that his name was to be in the same-size letters as Dorsey's. But the theater, MGM's showcase Manhattan theater, violated the agreement and printed Jackie's name about one-third the size of Dorsey's in newspaper advertising.

Now billing is a performer's bank account; a loss of billing can mean bankruptcy to a performer, even the most forgiving of them. Gleason refused to work the Capitol because it violated his contract in the newspaper ads. He took a job at the Chanticleer in Baltimore instead. It was hardly the Capitol, but once again, the fates were working for Jackie. The club had a chorus line that was a nightclub rarity—the girls could really dance.

"If I ever hit it big," Jackie told Willie, "I'm going to hire that choreographer." The choreographer was June Taylor, the only choreographer Gleason would ever use on television in later years.

In those postwar years, anyone would tell you that Jackie was the best "table comedian" in the business. That means he was a riot at Toots Shor's for free, but he couldn't command the five thousand a week that Milton Berle and Joe E. Lewis got at the big clubs like the Copacabana in New York. Other comedians of that era, who don't want their names used because they are good friends of Jackie's, say that in those days Jackie had everything but an act. No one could ad-lib better than Jackie, except Berle, but even Berle wouldn't go into a big club without a well-rehearsed act, one that was surefire.

Lack of an act didn't faze Jackie, as long as he could louse up his pigeon, Toots Shor. The big circular bar in the front of Toots' saloon was Jackie's home away from home. He did all his drinking and all his heckling of Toots' food from that favorite corner barstool. (Once he yelled at the top of his voice to Eddie Arcaro, the great jockey, who was sitting on the far side of the room: "Eddie, do you know what you are eating now, you rode yesterday at Belmont?")

Sometimes Toots would get peeved at Jackie and bar him from the place for a week or two, especially when Jackie ordered a truckload of horse manure and had it dumped on the sidewalk in front of the restaurant. The reason is long forgotten, but Jackie thinks it had something to do with Toots being full of horseshit.

Often in those days, Jackie would come into Toots' eating a big pizza he had bought at some Italian café down the street. The customers loved it because it made up for a lack of floor show.

Jackie always signed his tab but paid all tips in cash. "I once felt that I had run up too big a tab and told Toots I couldn't sign anymore. He told me to sign his name. Then I borrowed a twenty from him and gave it to the captain and waiter, apologizing, 'Hey, I personally am always good for a C-note, but you guys all know how cheap Toots is.'"

The big party of the year in Toots' place was always his birthday, which, in 1947, happened to fall on a Friday. Jackie shopped around for an unusual gift and finally came up with a live pig he bought from a meat packer. It was supposed to be a surprise, so he got some workmen to take the live pig in a box crate down into the basement. Unfortunately, the workmen got to some booze first and dropped the pig, breaking its neck. The SPCA couldn't remove the dead carcass since it was a weekend, and by Saturday night, the restaurant had a stench that drove off half the customers. Gleason sat through it all at the bar, urging those customers who stayed to try the pork chops. "They're freshly dressed in our own cellars."

The general public really didn't know Gleason that well, but he was a celebrity with the Broadway crowd. In January of 1947, Walter Winchell plugged him in his column after seeing him one night at the Club 18. "Funniest new comic on the block," wrote Winchell, whose column was Broadway gospel. It's hard to imagine today what a plug in Winchell's column could do for a new performer in those days. All of show business read Hearst's *Daily Mirror* for Winchell's column. Even Ed Sullivan, whose *Daily News* Broadway column had three times the circulation, could not wield power like Winchell.

That little plug in Winchell's column got Gleason into one of Manhattan's major nightspots—Billy Rose's Diamond Horseshoe. The two-week stand paid $3,500 per week, the biggest nightclub money Jackie had ever gotten.

Following that engagement, he did a radio show on WOR, Newark, for a measly $150. When Willie Webber went to collect the check, as managers and agents do, he found out that Gleason had already taken it all in advance. Life and career were a rollercoaster for Jackie, as always. Gleason had given the money to Joe Harrison, the maître d' at Toots', as a tip.

Jackie would ad-lib with anyone, even such a master as Milton Berle, king of the ad-libbers. They took each other on one night at Toots' bar, and it was a standoff. Everybody thought the two were enemies after that. No way. A few weeks after that insult contest, Gleason needed a thousand bucks, and Milton couldn't get it out of his pocket fast enough. The two legendary comics have had their differences over the years but they have remained good friends and have great respect for each other.

In 1948, Willie Webber convinced Jackie he could do no more for him. (He didn't tell him that the commissions either were too small or nonexistent because Jackie always borrowed ahead on his salary. Willie eventually got all the money Jackie owed him.) About the time Willie and Jackie split, George ("Bullets") Durgom left the band business and went into personal management. Jackie, who once had tried to hire Bullets as a stooge when Bullets was road manager for Tommy Dorsey, now wanted no one else to book him. And, most importantly, a medium that would make Gleason a superstar was just getting its start—television.

Berle was already television's number-one star in 1948 with his "Texaco Star Theater." A few months after Berle went on the air, Ed Sullivan, whose only show business experience was writing about it, was hosting a variety show. Ed looked like a bad embalming job, but he lasted twenty-five years on television. (Once Sullivan was in the audience of Berle's show. Sullivan made a practice of introducing celebrities in the audience of his own show, so Berle fol-

□

lowed suit. "Ladies and Gentlemen," said Milton from the stage. "I'd like to introduce Ed Sullivan and his lovely widow, Sylvia.")

Bullets' first job for Jackie was a spot on the Sullivan show in the fall of 1948. Gleason did a funny routine about a guy frustrated by playing a pinball machine. It was a riot, and Sullivan was after Bullets immediately to set a return date for Gleason.

But back in Hollywood, writer Irving Brecher had seen the Sullivan kinescope—a primitive picture taken from the television tube in those early days. Brecher was the creator of one of radio's biggest hit shows, "The Life of Riley." It starred the late William Bendix as the nincompoop husband Chester Riley.

In 1948, Brecher had sold the series to television, but he couldn't get Bendix, who was under contract to RKO Pictures for movies. In its early days, television was seen as the plague by moviemakers, and Howard Hughes, boss of RKO, would not allow Bendix to do the television version of "Riley." Howard was not being unusually small-minded; every movie studio in town practiced the same ban. Many studios even banned TV sets on the lot.

When Brecher saw Gleason on that Sullivan kinescope, he knew he had his television Riley. He and Bullets went into immediate negotiations while Jackie did a nightclub show in Pittsburgh.

There one night over some Paddy's Irish whiskey, a priest caught Jackie in a sentimental mood. It was just before Christmas of 1948, and the priest convinced Jackie he should go back to his wife and children. It was the children, the priest argued, who were being hurt the most by the estrangement of the mother and father.

True, Jackie missed his wife and kids. They bickered a

□

lot, but it was Gen to whom Jackie could retreat and be soothed. He told her about his talk with the priest in Pittsburgh and she agreed to take him back.

"We even got married again. This time by Father Moose McCormick at St. Gregory's Church in Brooklyn. All during the ceremony, I had misgivings because there were some workmen outside building a scaffolding. I kept thinking all this pounding and hammering was the devil trying to tell me not to get married again."

But remarried they were, and when Jackie went out to Hollywood early in 1949 to do "The Life of Riley," the Gleasons all went out there as one big happy Catholic family. Jackie even started going to mass every morning with Gen. They set up housekeeping in an apartment on Sycamore Street, right in the heart of Hollywood.

Daughter Geraldine recalls: "I remember that we had the only television set on the block. That fall of 1949, everybody used to come to our house to watch our set, especially Dad's show. I was about ten then and I soon found out what my father did for a living. I remember Linda and I went to the Cathedral school with John Wayne's two youngest, Patrick and Melinda."

It was inevitable that Gen would become pals with Josie Wayne, Duke's first wife, who, like Gen, was a very devout Catholic. Another close friend of these two was the silent movie star, Marion Davies. This was surprising, though, because Marion was a drinker in the tradition of Wayne and Gleason.

"Marion was brought up a Catholic and she was impressed by Gen, the most devout Catholic I have ever known," says Jackie. "She couldn't help but be impressed. Gen makes Dolores (Mrs. Bob) Hope look like an atheist."

□

Gleason, meanwhile, wasn't behaving like an altar boy. Leonard Stern, later to become one of Jackie's writers in the early CBS years, recalls how he first met Jackie in Las Vegas in 1949, around the time Gleason came west for "The Life of Riley."

"I was a screenwriter in those days writing for Abbott and Costello out at Universal and I went up to Las Vegas to catch Jackie at the El Rancho Vegas. He was on the bill with Chaz Chase [one of the great pantomime comics who was as big a favorite in Paris and London as he was in New York].

"Jackie was never funnier than he was when he performed with Chaz. He built his act around Chaz, who had an outrageous act. Chaz used to eat cigarettes, chew his collar, his shirtfront, and do a crazy dance where he kept slipping. Jackie would give Ralph Kramden reactions to Chaz, long before we or Jackie knew there was going to be a Ralph Kramden.

"I can't remember exactly how Jackie and I met but I remember that I had saved one hundred twenty-five dollars, maybe two hundred fifty, for the trip. Jackie suggested that we pool our money and gamble in the casino. I was only twenty-two then and had never gambled in my life.

"Jackie took our money to the crap table and rolled the dice. He attracted a big crowd at the table because before he rolled the dice, he would go way back to the end of the casino and then, with elephantine steps, run up to the crap table and yell 'Load it on.' He had a remarkable run with the dice and finally some guy next to me said: 'You guys got about ten thousand dollars there, why don't you quit and cash in?'

"I went up to Jackie and told him we ought to quit. He

said, 'Don't stop me. You're jinxing me.' He kept on rolling and rolling with that same long run. I managed to siphon off some chips until I had about six hundred worth—and that was all.

"Next day, Jackie asked me how much we won. I told him six hundred dollars. 'That's wonderful,' he said. Then I told him that we were once ten thousand ahead. 'Why in the hell didn't you stop me?' he said.

"I then realized he was smashed and didn't remember a damn thing about the crap game."

Jackie's friends were a little hard for any wife to take. One was Polly Adler, who ran New York's most famous whorehouse until the vice squad chased her out of town. She set up shop in Hollywood and brought some of her Manhattan girls with her. Polly had taken a liking to Jackie when he was at the Club 18, and he often went up to her whorehouse—because it had a great bar.

"I never jumped on any of her girls. I just liked the atmosphere of her bar. And I wasn't the only one. Jack Dempsey (heavyweight champion 1919–26), and Max Baer (heavyweight titleholder 1934–35) both were regulars at Polly's. Max even used to bring his girlfriend up there to drink. Even Johnny Broderick, the tough New York cop who had every hoodlum in town scared of him, hung out there. The place had a certain ambience." (In the fifties, after Polly had graduated from UCLA, she wrote a best-selling book about her life as a famous madam. It had a wonderful title—*A House Is Not a Home*. She autographed a copy to Gleason with "Never a patient, always a friend.")

One day in Hollywood, after both he and Polly had moved there, Jackie got a phone call. Gen answered and told Jackie knowingly, "Pearl is on the phone." For some

strange reason, Polly always used the code name Pearl
when calling gentlemen friends. Gen was well aware who
Pearl was. She had called too many times before.

"She calls this one night when we were living on
Orange Street in Hollywood. [Jackie must have had trouble
finding the house at night; he lived on Sycamore, one street
removed from Orange.] And she invited me to a Christmas
party she was giving for the girls. Now, Polly and her girls
knew hardly anyone in town, outside of customers. I really
was her only friend in Hollywood. There was no way I
could turn down that invitation."

Gen raised holy hell. She couldn't understand how
Jackie could hang around a whorehouse and remain a good
Catholic. Jackie went to the party anyway.

"Well," Jackie recalls. "It was the damnedest party I
ever went to. I sat at the head of the table and Polly sat at
the other end. We all sang Christmas carols and her girls,
all gorgeous, were dressed in crinolines. Hell, it was more
like May Day in Vassar than a party in a whorehouse."
Making Gen believe that was of course impossible.

There were other friendships that weren't quite as innocent. Jack Philbin, who worked for Bullets Durgom, introduced Jackie to a particularly luscious Warner Bros.
starlet and gave Jackie the key to his house in the Hollywood Hills. He even called a cab and put Jackie and the
girl in it and gave the cabdriver the address. After Jackie
and the girl had consumed all of Philbin's booze and had
had a friendly little romp in the hay, the girl started moaning that she was late for a date with her fiancé. No problem, except Jackie didn't know where in the hell he was.

He called Philbin, but he wasn't in the office. A secretary didn't know where Philbin lived, so Jackie asked for
Bullets. He was in New York at the Plaza Hotel. Jackie

called there and got Bullets on the phone. "Where does Philbin live?" he asked.

"On Woodrow Wilson Drive, you dumb son of a bitch. Are you drunk again?"

Jackie knew the street now. All he had to do was look on the front porch for the street number. A cab was called and the girl didn't disappoint the guy she was going to marry. (In fact, she is still married to him.)

As for "The Life of Riley," the cast rehearsed all week and then filmed the show in one day. People who took weeks to make movies, and lucky if they got three minutes of film a day, used to watch Gleason and the other actors in amazement. But the fast pace of the television series didn't do much for the quality of the show. Jackie feels that all it did for his career was buy groceries and booze and pay the rent.

"In 1949, all people cared about seeing was that picture that floated through the air and landed in your living room on a seven-inch screen. Made no difference whether the show was bad or good; just that it got there was miracle enough."

Bullets has a different opinion. "Jackie is one of the most colorful performers in the history of show business, but in the tradition of John Barrymore, Errol Flynn and W. C. Fields. That meant he drank colorfully. It also meant that he was a hard sell. I know he has never missed a show because of his drinking, but tell that to a nightclub owner. He has enough drunks for customers. He doesn't want to be paying for a star who drinks.

"'The Life of Riley' proved one thing—that Jackie was a highly professional performer who worked hard and, when he wasn't working, played hard. He never was a hard sell after that show."

□

83

Another advantage of "Riley" was its national exposure. The series wasn't all that great, but Gleason was, and it proved that he could carry a show. Never again would Gleason be just a Broadway comic or a Hollywood featured player.

They knew who he was in Sheboygan now.

▪ 8 ▪
AND
AWAY
WE
GO!

In the spring of 1950, Jackie and his family went back to New York by train, his one season with "The Life of Riley" finished. Whether he knew it or not, Jackie had found the medium that was made for him. Even on the train trip—by Santa Fe Super Chief to Chicago and New York Central 20th Century Limited to New York—it seemed that everyone knew him. Some even called him "Chester," the first name of Riley in the television show. And in New York, he could stroll down Fifth Avenue and everybody would call him by name. In one short year, he had become a national celebrity.

All of this was great for Jackie's ego, but oddly, it never really dawned on Jackie that this new invention was his entrée to superstardom; he didn't even buy a TV set

□

when he got back to New York. He was more interested in drinking with Toots Shor.

"I never bought a set in New York because I was never home to watch it. I just didn't think about it until later. I sometimes would catch a wrestling match in a bar but I really thought television was something that distracted from my drinking. It interfered with the good fellowship of conversation at the bar."

The more he made life miserable for his pal Toots, the happier Jackie was. Toots had a phobia about elevators and Jackie knew it. Now, no one can live in New York and avoid elevators, even if they scare the hell out of you. Jackie used to lie in wait for Toots to visit his lawyer's office on the twelfth floor of a Manhattan skyscraper. Jackie knew how to pull the switch that would stop the elevator, usually between the fourth and fifth floor. You could hear Toots scream over all mid-Manhattan.

Jackie's marriage had been somewhat smoother in California, but as soon as he got back to New York, it was obvious that he was not about to reform. He came home at dawn, usually drunk, and the arguments would start. He moved into the Hotel Edison this time, along with Max Kaminsky's Dixieland Band. The other tenants complained they couldn't sleep with Max's boys blasting "Way Down Yonder in New Orleans" at 5 A.M.

In desperation, Jackie called Sammy Lewis in Hollywood and said he wanted to work Slapsy Maxie's again. Lewis happily sent him the train fare, and Gleason once again was a major hit at Slapsy's. Even Fanny Brice and Charlie Chaplin became fans. Hollywood producers and directors told him he was the funniest man alive by night, but they did little or nothing for him by day. The movies still didn't know how to use Gleason. His big movie role of 1950 was as a blue-eyed Arabian camel driver in a movie starring Richard Greene and Yvonne De Carlo called *The Desert Hawk*. As for his interest in television, Jackie had left New York, the center of the infant medium, and gone off to Hollywood.

Jackie was still doing the town every night with his co-stars from *Navy Blues,* Jack Oakie, Jack Haley, Jack Carson and his old burlesque pal, the hard-drinking Rags Ragland. Martha Raye was still another drinking buddy.

Back in New York, three networks were emerging as television powerhouses: NBC, CBS and Dumont. ABC had not yet become the force it eventually would. Dumont, which beamed mostly to the big cities, was named after one of television's early pioneers. It had a hot variety show called "Cavalcade of Stars," with Jack Carter, then a young comic, as the emcee. NBC, which had more money from its radio division, lured Carter away from Dumont.

Carter, still a working comedian-actor today, remembers: "I suggested Gleason as my replacement at Dumont. He was brash, moved fast on his feet. He did impressions as I had done and he was perfect to host the show. The bosses listened to me politely and then hired Jerry Lester."

Lester was a Las Vegas comic who stayed only a few months on the Dumont "Cavalcade." Once again, NBC offered more money and Jerry became the host of "Broadway Open House," the first late-night show, the forerunner for Steve Allen, Jack Paar and Johnny Carson's "Tonight" show.

The producer of the Dumont "Cavalcade" was an ex-singer named Milton Douglas. He had been a fan of Gleason's ever since he saw him do that hilarious Foreign Legion sketch in *Along Fifth Avenue.* The play hadn't run very long on Broadway, but Gleason's show-stopping scene had etched itself on Douglas' memory.

□

87

Douglas knew that Gleason was working in Hollywood, so he asked one of the sponsor's lawyers to check him out. (Whelan Drug, which also owned United Cigar Stores, was the sponsor.) While the lawyer, on a business trip to the West Coast, caught Gleason at Slapsy Maxie's, Douglas surprisingly approached Peter Donald, a low-profile wit who was one of TV's early comedians, to host "Cavalcade of Stars."

Donald, a more subtle type of comedian, knew that he wasn't right for the job, and turned it down. He even suggested Gleason to his agent, William Morris, but the Morris office was not about to tout Gleason. By now, Bullets had signed on with their rival, MCA.

And next, the Whelan Drug lawyer called Douglas. He had seen Jackie's act at Slapsy's and had decided that Gleason was the funniest man in the business, and perfect to host "Cavalcade." He told Douglas, "Sign him, quick. He's our man." And that's all that Douglas, desperately searching for a host, needed to hear.

Meanwhile, Jackie, not knowing what was going on, brought Gen and the kids out to Hollywood. He was trying his damnedest to keep his marriage intact, hopeless as it appeared to be. The Gleason family moved in with Jack and Flo Haley. (To this day, both Linda and Geraldine speak of the Haleys as "Aunt Flo" and "Uncle Jack.")

The family was hardly together again before Bullets told Gleason he was wanted for a two-week guest appearance on the Dumont show. The pay was only $750 per week, little more than he was getting from Sammy Lewis at Slapsy's. But once again, Jackie got on the Super Chief and left his family in Hollywood. Sammy and Ben Blue, a fellow comic at Slapsy's, went with Jackie down to Los Angeles' Union Station.

Lewis recalls that the last words Jackie yelled, as the

luxurious all-Pullman train pulled out of the station, were: "See you in two weeks, Sambo."

It was late summer of 1950. Jackie would not return to Los Angeles until 1952, and then only on vacation, as the biggest star of television.

When Gleason joined "Cavalcade of Stars" on July 8, 1950, the TV show already had two good comedy writers in Arne Rosen and Coleman Jacoby. At Slapsy's, Gleason had become friendly with MGM contract writer (the "Thin Man" series) Harry Crane. Crane, a habitué of Slapsy's, used to give Gleason his stage call by yelling: "They have just fired on Fort Sumter." Somehow this broke Gleason up, and he and Crane became drinking buddies.

Gleason's two weeks on "Cavalcade' became four and then he graduated to the whole season. Sometime during that first year, Crane took a trip east and Gleason immediately hired him and made him head writer. Apparently, this didn't set too well with the other writers, who left for more lucrative contracts on rival networks. Harry, for his first show, found himself not only as head writer, but as only writer. Bullets Durgom completed negotiations with Harry on a Tuesday and told him he would have to work fast. Airtime was the coming Friday, three days away. Crane remembers that first show:

"I went up to Jackie's apartment this first day and it sounded like Basie live. Dixieland bands were playing. Broads were all over the place smooching guys. It was Sodom and Gomorrah in overtime.

"I walk into this cold, and say, 'Jackie, we gotta talk about the script. There's sets to be built.' He says, 'Grab a broad and some booze and we'll talk Thursday.' Now, Thursday is twenty-four hours before airtime. Nothing to do but come back Thursday. This time the apartment looked like a suicide pact. Bodies passed out, strewn all over the apartment. I leave, and as I walk through the lobby, mothers grab me. 'My daughter's up there. Is she still alive?'

"Later that same day, I go back. Snap! Crackle! Pop! The party's on again. Everybody is dancing. Max Kaminsky's band is playing 'Back Home in Indiana' and I wish I was. Gleason is dancing steps that haven't been invented yet. No chance to talk script, so I left again.

"There's only one thing I can do. Milton Douglas is yelling for something on paper, so I write a Reggie Van Gleason the Third, a Joe the Bartender and a Poor Soul in such a way that only the barest of sets will be needed, something that can be built in an hour or two. These were all people Gleason had invented somewhere along the line in nightclubs and stage shows. No problem.

"On Friday, just a few hours before airtime, Jackie said he would take a look at what I had written. He glances at my script for a couple minutes, hands it back and says, 'Gotcha, pal.'

"Gotcha, pal? What the hell kind of show have I got myself into? I go back to the set. All the other actors are in a panic. They don't know what the hell they are going to do. No rehearsals. No chance to study the script. No nothing. Finally, Jackie shows up about an hour before airtime. The other actors are all over him, screaming, 'What the hell do we do? What the hell do we say?'

"Jackie has a stock answer for everyone: 'Every man for himself.' Every man for himself? On a live show that's going on the air in minutes to twenty million people? I ducked out. I didn't have the stomach or heart to watch a catastrophe. I went to the bar next door to the Adelphi Theater on West Fifty-fourth Street. I ordered doubles. Set 'em up in the next alley. The bar television was turned to the Gleason show. I couldn't believe what I saw. Gleason, who had just glanced at my script, was doing every line perfect. He didn't miss or flub a word. He was hilarious. Everybody in the bar was laughing their heads off. What had been absolute chaos only an hour ago now was comedy at its finest. I had to be working with a genius. At least, he was a comic like I had never worked with before and I had worked with some crazy comics, Red Skelton to name one."

Before Crane took over as head writer, Arne Rosen and Coleman Jacoby wrote a Reggie Van Gleason sketch—the playboy character Gleason had invented for *Along Fifth Avenue*—in which another comedy actor was needed. These two writers, who got their start in radio, knew of a radio actor now working in television on comedian Morey Amsterdam's show. The actor's name was Art Carney.

The Reggie sketch had the rich playboy Reggie being photographed by a prissy, almost effeminate, photographer for a "Man of Distinction" ad plugging booze. The sketch was somewhat loosely based on Red Skelton's Guzzler's Gin routine, one of the redheaded clown's most famous. In it, Red played a movie disc jockey introducing old movies on the Late Night Show. In between, he demonstrated the sponsor's product—Guzzler's Gin—by drinking it during commercial breaks. By the end of the movie, Red was gloriously and uproariously drunk.

The Gleason version had Reggie drinking from the sponsor's bottle and then offering the photographer a drink. By the end of the photo session, Gleason was taking a photo of Carney and both of them were loaded. It was funny, and historic; in this sketch, Laurel had found his Hardy, and vice versa.

Let Carney recall that sketch: "I had never heard of Gleason before we did the sketch, but I'm telling you, we clicked like we had been doing an act together for years. Whatever he gave to me, I gave back to him in spades. It was incredible the way we hit it off."

Milton Douglas saw the remarkable chemistry between the two and had Carney back time after time. There never was a written contract for Carney, just a verbal understanding.

"Once Jackie called me, and said, 'It's nice working with you.'"

All of which brings us up to Jackie Gleason's most famous character, another he created for himself. This was weeks later, during the fall of 1950.

"I had this idea for a long time," Jackie recalls. "I knew a thousand couples like these in Brooklyn. It was the loudmouth husband, like in the George Kelly play *The Show-Off*, with a wife who is a hell of a lot smarter than her husband. My neighborhood was filled with them.

"I told the idea to my writers, Harry Crane and Joe Bigelow. I wanted something believable, something the working stiffs could all identify with."

Harry immediately came up with the title "The Beast." Jackie didn't like it. The guy was no beast, even though he was always fighting with his wife. He really loved her and Jackie wanted each show to end happily with a hug and a kiss. "You're the greatest" was the tag line he wanted.

More titles were kicked around. "The Lovers," Jackie said, was getting close. He wanted an instant tag that would let the viewers know they were married. Jackie himself came up with the everlasting title "The Honeymooners." Gleason had not only created the show and its title, he also designed the crummy flat the couple lived in, with its dripping icebox, kitchen table and sink and little gas range.

"Hell, I lived in enough of these joints to know what

□

they looked like," said Jackie. The kitchen of Ralph and Alice Kramden looked pretty much like the one Jackie lived in with his mother at 358 Chauncey Street in the Bushwick section of Brooklyn. Crane drafted a script but set it in Bensonhurst, because he thought it would be a better-sounding neighborhood for television. (Harry himself came from Brownsville, also in Brooklyn.)

Right away, Jackie knew whom he wanted to play Alice, the wife—Pert Kelton. Pert had once been a leading lady for Charlie Chaplin in movies, and she had played brassy wives on the stage. She was ideal casting. The first "Honeymooners" sketch had only Jackie and Pert as principals. In it, Ralph Kramden comes home from a hard day's work driving a bus. Alice yells at him to go down to the store and get some bread for supper. "You mean, you want me to go down and buy some bread? What have you been doing all day?"

Alice picks up a pie she has been baking and throws it at Ralph. He ducks and the pie goes out the window. A knock on the door and the neighborhood cop shows up with pie on his face. It was Art Carney. It was a funny sketch back there in the early part of 1951 when it got on the air, just for a few minutes, and it caused the switchboard at the old Dumont studio (where the New York Hilton now stands) to light up like a Christmas tree. Jack Lescoulie, an old drinking buddy of Jackie's from Toots Shor's, who was the announcer on the show, told Harry, "You guys will have to come up with that sketch every month."

June Taylor, the choreographer Jackie had vowed to hire when he first met her at the Chanticleer in Baltimore back in 1946, then made the most prophetic remark: "Don't you mean every week?"

Both Crane and Bigelow, and most of all Jackie, knew

□

that Carney had to become a regular in "The Honey-mooners." No one could ignore the great chemistry that existed between Carney and Gleason. They were the greatest teaming since Smith and Dale, the funny team of the twenties and thirties who inspired Neil Simon's smash play *The Sunshine Boys.*

Back in those early days of television, characters in situation comedies all lived in middle-class suburbia or better; only Gleason would come up with life in a slum. It took a lot of guts, but it all worked, because the Kramdens and the Nortons were real people with whom many in the United States could identify.

Because they were poor, Ralph and Ed were always trying some get-rich-quick scheme. None ever worked, and Alice let her husband know it. "Forget it, Ralph" was her trademark line. (Had any of the schemes worked, "The Honeymooners" would have had to become another show entirely, set in Westchester County, perhaps, and called "Ralph Knows Best.")

Even today, Crane is amazed at how Gleason used to memorize "The Honeymooners" scripts.

"I'd go over to his apartment. He would still be in bed, looking like a fighter who had just gotten off the canvas. I'd give him a copy of the script and then start reading all the parts. He would start shaving with his copy lying on the bathroom sink. As I read all the parts, he would glance down at his copy, never stopping with the razor. By the time he had shaved himself, he not only knew his part but everybody else's. It took all of two minutes."

Gleason claims that the funniest script of that 1951 winter season was completely ad-libbed.

"I threw the script in the wastebasket and got Pert and Carney in my office. I told Pert to put some paper in a typewriter. She wrote the title on top of the page. We were all drinking pretty good in those days, so when it came time to go on the air, all we had on paper was the title.

"So I said to Art to wait outside when we got on the air. Pert and I would start a fight and Art would then come in and try to break it up. And we would go on from there. We ad-libbed the whole damn thing. I still have people come up to me today and tell me how funny that show was."

·9·
JACKIE GLEASON, MILLIONAIRE

In 1951, Jackie Gleason was making $1,000 a week as host of Dumont's "Cavalcade of Stars" and could command ten times that in guest appearances. But it was when he did a guest shot—for free—with an old pal from New Jersey that he became a millionaire.

Frank Sinatra, who once sang for nothing himself, just to be heard on Jersey radio stations, was making $10,000 a week—1951's highest television salary—when he asked Gleason to appear on his show.

"The Frank Sinatra Show" was taped in New York, even though Frank was living in Beverly Hills at the time. It was one of the biggest hits of 1951. Historically, it introduced Sinatra the performer, as we know him today, rather than just Sinatra the singer. Midway in the show, Frank used to sit on a stool and sip tea between patter with the audience. (In Frank's case, it actually *was* tea, because that beverage soothes the vocal cords. Later, Gleason would do the same thing with coffee—the only 100 proof coffee in existence.) Frank's patter was so good that CBS-TV used his live laughs for situation-comedy sound tracks for years afterward.

The show was a long commute for Frank, and it was tough to leave someone like Ava Gardner, then one of the screen's great beauties, for a few days each week. By January 1952, Frank was devoting less time to the show, which worried the CBS brass.

One live taping night in New York, Frank's plane from the West Coast arrived only a few hours before airtime. Director Jack Donahue put him on before a plain black curtain and he sang only standards, mostly Cole Porter, from his nightclub book. It was a classic show because of its utter simplicity. It was such a hit, in fact, that CBS renewed him for thirteen more weeks that very night. But the brass was really worried—what if the plane hadn't made it?

Donahue proposed to Frank that he use a comedian as a guest star, strictly as a back-up precaution. Frank had only one choice. Jackie remembers: "It was Frank himself who asked me to appear with him, not the network. For my first entrance, I came down the aisle with about a half dozen beautiful girls on either side of me. I was beating them off with a cane. I came onstage, interrupted Frank's song and we hit it off like Abbott and Costello. Frank is a very funny guy himself—and I knew that from our long friendship. I refused to take a cent from him." (Actually, due to union rules, Gleason got $250, AFTRA (American Federation of Television and Radio Artists) scale for a network appearance then.)

The show was such a smash that Frank insisted that

Gleason be rewarded. The next time Gleason appeared on the show, a few weeks later, in mid-season 1952, Frank took him out to the stage alley and showed him the biggest Cadillac limousine anyone had ever seen. Frank had bought it as a gift from some undertaker he knew over in New Jersey for five thousand bucks. On it was a gold-leaf emblem that read: "From F.S. to J.G. with love." To accent the message, a heart-shaped insignia backed it.

As an added touch, there was Toots Shor in a chauffeur's cap, ready to take Frank and Jackie anyplace. Pal Judy Garland was appearing at the famous Palace in Times Square, so off they went to see Judy's show.

Toots obviously had had a few drinks at his bar before he put on the chauffeur's cap, and while driving through the heavy traffic in Times Square Toots almost ran down a pedestrian. The guy, spotting Sinatra and Gleason in the back seat, clenched his fist and yelled, "You rich cocksuckers!"

"For some strange reason," Jackie recalls, "that upset me. I never rode in or drove the car after that. I don't know what the hell happened to it."

Jackie did six shows with Frank—which did not conflict with his weekly show on Dumont—during the winter of 1952. Jackie didn't know it, but those CBS guest spots with Frank produced a VIP fan—Bill Paley, the founder of CBS.

Paley immediately sent word to his number-two man, Hubbell Robinson: "Get us Gleason." Robinson was better known for his knowledge of Civil War history than anything else. He was a well-tailored Ivy Leaguer, the epitome of the successful TV executive. He had never seen Gleason, not even on the Sinatra show, over which he was the nominal boss.

But what Paley wanted, Paley got. Robinson negotiated with Bullets Durgom and MCA's finest deal makers, and signed Gleason in September of 1952 to a two-year, $11 million contract, the biggest ever in the history of television up to that time. All Gleason had to do was to deliver a weekly variety show lasting one hour on Saturday nights. Jackie read the contract literally and, like Berle before him, took complete command of writing, producing, directing, editing, lighting, choreography, music and everything else. No stars, before or since, have ever so completely run their own shows as Berle and Gleason did.

Jackie also got some fringe benefits, such as a fabulous house, paid for by CBS, located in Peekskill, up the Hudson River. The house was round because Jackie reasoned that such a shape would make it easier to have a bar no farther away than twenty feet from any given spot in the house. George Jessel, on his first visit there, called it "a bar with a house built in." Jackie thought that any bar farther away than twenty feet was in outer space.

The contract was the talk of the trade and the nation in 1952. The night before the signing, Jackie, singer Johnny Ray and famed artist Salvador Dali went out on the town and got uproariously drunk, getting home at 5 A.M. At the contract signing ceremony in Paley's office that day, Jackie fell asleep in the middle of the luncheon.

"Hey," Paley is reported to have said, "if that is his attitude, give him what he wants."

Gleason will deny that he actually *is* Reggie Van Gleason, but the first thing he asked for after the signing that September day was a $75,000 advance—which he promptly got. And promptly spent. He took the money, moved out of his Fifty-second Street apartment and leased the two most luxurious penthouses atop the Park Sheraton hotel—$25,000 for the first year. With the other $50,000— which bought a lot in 1952—he ripped out walls, had a top interior decorator redo the penthouses and created the damnedest television headquarters anyone had ever seen for the new CBS-TV "Jackie Gleason Show." His only concession to humility was to list "jackie gleason enterprises" in lower-case type.

Up to this time, television headquarters were dingy production offices, usually in dingy buildings. Gleason's headquarters made Paley's look like a slum. To NBC-TV executives, the Gleason palace looked like the place they hoped to go to when they died. Jackie's personal headquarters, really his living quarters, were like something out of the *Arabian Nights*—a sultan's palace.

His television set was imbedded into the ceiling above an emperor-sized—not king-sized—bed. Naturally, a huge pool table dominated the living room, the ultimate status symbol for the onetime kid pool-hustler from Brooklyn. Writers had a separate suite, although they seldom ever saw the star, but their suite was near the producer's. June Taylor, the choreographer, had a dance studio complete with mirrors and ballet barres.

Naturally, there were plenty of the sort of bars Jackie preferred, plus a Chinese houseboy who doubled as a bartender. The main room was basilica-sized, with two-story windows that overlooked Central Park, which served as Jackie's private garden. Above a huge fireplace that burned trees, instead of mere logs, hung an oversized, beaming portrait of Reggie Van Gleason the Third in a World War I doughboy's uniform. Beneath it was a gold plate inscribed "Our Founder." And the place was filled, at all times, with beautiful showgirls, dancers and piles of Chinese food, making it look like the banquet scene from *The King and I*. (Jackie's marriage was in its final throes, and Gen and the girls, though living in New York, had no part of this setup. They were ensconced off Central Park.)

Since much of the summer of 1952 was a transition period between the end of Jackie's contract with Dumont and his signing with CBS, he took his troupe on the road for a series of personal appearances. First they played a theater in Pittsburgh, and then they took the train for Chicago. On the overnight train ride, Pert Kelton got deathly ill. An old trouper, believing all that stuff about the show must go on, Pert did four shows in Chicago. She collapsed on the fourth and was rushed to a hospital. She had suffered a coronary thrombosis.

"Pert, who was damn good as Alice Kramden, never played her again after that setback," says Jackie.

After Pert's illness, Jackie returned to New York and started preparing for the new fall TV season. (Although the CBS contract was not in effect until September, Jackie knew it was well in the works months before that.)

When not working on the TV show, he indulged in his great hobby—lousing up Toots Shor. One of the benefits Jackie derived from Frank's television show during the 1951–52 season—aside from his becoming a millionaire—was Sinatra's role as a co-conspirator in the harassment of Toots.

Frank says he will never forget October 3, 1951, as long as he lives. That was the day the Brooklyn Dodgers and New York Giants met at the Polo Grounds in the final playoff game for the National League pennant. That morning Frank met Gleason at Toots' for a morning eye-opener. Immediately, the two started heckling Toots, who was doing his utmost to impress a distinguished early lunch customer—J. Edgar Hoover, head of the FBI.

Seeing that Toots was getting burned up and ready to toss out the two hecklers, Frank made amends by offering to take Toots, Hoover and Gleason to the Polo Grounds.

Leo Durocher, manager of the Giants and a buddy of Sinatra's, had given Frank four choice seats for the playoff game. Toots was overjoyed and so was Hoover. Gleason, although a Dodger fan, was gulping a drink and was really in no mood to leave the bar and fight all that traffic. Toots solved that by ordering a limousine and stocking it with booze and food.

Sinatra remembers: "We pile into that limousine, already feeling no pain, especially Gleason. Jackie guzzled booze all the way to the Polo Grounds and ate most of the food. When we get to the Polo Grounds, Gleason switches to hot dogs and beer. Comes the last half of the ninth and the game is really crucial. Fans are going wild, especially the Giant fans, who were a special breed in New York. The Giants are behind 4–2 and Bobby Thomson comes to bat.

"Right at that exact moment, with the crowd screaming, Gleason throws up on me. Here is one of the all-time classic games that people still talk about and I am right in the stadium and I don't see Bobby Thomson hit that home run. I just heard the Giant fans going wild around us. Only Gleason, a Brooklyn fan, would get sick at a time like that.

"Hoover was very solicitous. He lent me his handkerchief to wipe myself off. But that's not the punch line.

"On the drive back to Toots', Gleason keeps muttering to the chauffeur to pull over to the side of the road saying, 'Let's throw this bum Sinatra out of here. He's smelling up the limo.'"

A year later, in October of 1952, to be precise, Gleason and Sinatra were drinking in Jimmy Ryan's, a jazz restaurant in Manhattan. Sitting at the bar were two bona fide bobby-soxers who kept ogling Sinatra, the bobby-soxers' delight in those days. The girls apparently had legal IDs, or else they wouldn't have been at the bar, but Jackie recalls that they both looked sixteen or seventeen at most.

Gleason's scheming mind, as it related to Toots, got a brilliant idea, which he immediately proposed to Frank. Why not take these young chicks back to Toots' saloon and tell him all four were going to Virginia Beach for a weekend of partying? Frank, equally mischievous, loved it.

Gleason and Frank invited the girls to join them at their table. Naturally, they were thrilled and overwhelmed. The Virginia Beach weekend was proposed and the girls said they would go to their apartment right away and pack. Before too long, they were back with two hatboxes filled with clothes. The gag was on and all four took a cab over to Toots' place.

"Well, when we came into the bar and Toots spotted these young broads, he went crazy," Jackie recalls. "And when we told him we were taking them to Virginia Beach, he went even crazier. First, he started to reason with us that both our careers would be ruined. 'You'll get arrested for the Mann Act,' he screamed. 'So what,' I answered. 'We'll get a couple years in jail and these girls will only be eighteen when we get out.' That did it. Toots was on the phone, calling every airline and charter service in town, warning them all they would be liable if they flew us to Virginia Beach or anyplace else."

Jackie and Frank kept pouring it on, acting lovey-dovey with the girls. It wasn't hard to do; Jackie remembers both as quite beautiful, even if they were bobby-soxers. Toots was a mental case as the four walked out arm-in-arm, headed ostensibly for Virginia Beach.

They went back, instead, to Jimmy Ryan's. The gag had worked on their favorite all-time pigeon, but what to tell the girls? Jackie convinced Frank, since he was the romantic attraction, to give them the sad news that it was all a gag.

Amazingly, the girls took it all quite well. "Just

think," one of them said, "we almost spent the weekend in Virginia Beach with Frank Sinatra and Jackie Gleason." (One can imagine those two girls telling that tale for years to their friends and neighbors, and maybe even to their own daughters, probably with no one believing them.)

Toots Shor, for all his outward veneer as a Manhattan saloon owner, and a sophisticated celebrity at that, was a sucker for any Gleason gag. The more outrageous the gag, the faster Toots would bite.

During the summer of 1952, while the New York Yankees were engaged in a hot race for the pennant, Gleason found another hard-drinking conspirator—the sensational rookie Mickey Mantle.

Joe DiMaggio had introduced Mantle to Gleason, and the home-run slugger soon became a regular at Toots' shop. Mickey was the reincarnation of the fast-living Babe Ruth, a drinker by day and a long ball hitter by night. (In Ruth's time, though, the hours were reversed; there was no night baseball.) Mickey would go along with any gag Gleason wanted to pull on Toots, and one day at the bar, Jackie and Mickey got into a terrible argument, completely staged.

Gleason invited Mantle to go into the men's room and fight it out. The two went into the lavatory and picked up wastebaskets and anything that was loose and threw it against the walls. Then they pounded on the doors, making one hell of a ruckus. Some poor guy sitting behind a closed toilet probably thought he was in the middle of a bomb raid.

After making all that noise inside, Gleason walked out with his shirt pulled out, his hair all mussed up and told Toots, "Better call the Yankees' doctor. I beat the hell out of Mickey. He's not playing any more this season."

Toots got on the phone and called the paramedics.

□

And then he looked up and saw Mantle coming out of the men's room, smiling. Toots knew he had been had once more.

"You crumb-bums," he yelled at Gleason and Mantle, ordering them out of the restaurant.

It's a wonder that the Yankees were so great in the early fifties; Whitey Ford, Roger Maris and Billy Martin were also regulars at Toots' bar. It was inevitable that Gleason and Martin would become friends.

In his youth, Jackie considered himself as good a bowler as a pool hustler. But he didn't know that Martin was better, and one fall day in 1952, Gleason challenged Martin to a bowling match for three hundred bucks. Toots was so elated, he offered to back Martin. Billy recalls that there was no need. He knew how good a bowler he was.

"The first game," Billy recalls, "I beat Jackie easily. He wanted to double the bet, so I rolled two hundred fifteen, good enough to win the six hundred bucks. Gleason still wanted more, and doubled the bet. Okay. I rolled three straight strikes and a spare. Gleason handed over the money and made an exit like he did that traveling music bit on television, 'Awa-a-a-ay I go!'"

The next night, since Gleason was in his baseball phase, he came into Toots' with a fungo bat (the light bat used to hit flies to outfielders in batting practice), a couple of baseball gloves and some balls. It was after midnight but DiMaggio was still there. Gleason and the Yankee Clipper took a cab to Central Park and Jackie hit flies to DiMaggio.

When they came back, Toots was crazy; no one, he said, goes into Central Park after midnight unless they have a Magnum .44 and couple of snarling Doberman pinschers. Toots asked them if they saw any muggers.

"About ten of them," said Jackie. "They all wanted

DiMaggio's autograph. It's safer to go in Central Park with Joe than it is with a squadron of cops."

Toots, as a drinker, was unusual. He was Jewish, and there just aren't many hard drinkers in the Jewish culture. Toots always prided himself in his ability to outdrink Gleason, a product of the Irish drinking tradition. And Jackie was always challenging Toots to drinking contests. Jackie knew he might lose, but he also knew that the challenge meant that all drinks would be on the house.

Sinatra loves to recall the night in 1952 when Toots drank Jackie right off a barstool into a big heap on the floor. Waiters and captains rushed to pick up the fallen giant, but Toots stopped them. "Let the bum lie there. It will teach that fat Irisher he can't drink with us Jew boys." Diners for the next half hour or so had to step over one of television's biggest stars to get to their tables.

Toots, when sober, was a kind, good-hearted host who would help out any friend in need. He would even let him eat and drink on credit, as he did with Gleason for many years. Drunk, Toots was something else. He had a bizarre habit, when drinking, of ordering people out of a place, whether it was his party or not. Sometimes he would shove and push people out of his own place at considerable cost, as most didn't ever have a chance to pay their tabs. Once he was drinking across the street at Club "21" when he came into his own pub and ordered everyone to evacuate. A priest was drinking at the bar. As Toots was pushing out his customers, he leaned over to the priest and said, "Not you, Father."

Bing Crosby, Humphrey Bogart, Jimmy Cagney, George Raft—all the Hollywood crowd used to hit Toots' place when they came to town. Bing, known to have taken a drink or two in his time, always met Gleason there. One day in 1952, Jackie and Bing drank through the cocktail hour and supper at Toots' and then went over to El Morocco, the ultra-chic watering hole, for a late-night drink.

"As soon as Bing walked into El Morocco," Jackie recalls, "the house band started playing 'Where the Blue of the Night Meets the Gold of the Day,' Bing's theme song. When Bing heard that, he walked up to the bandstand and started singing with them. By the time he was through, he had sung about twenty of the songs he had made famous through the years. What a night that was for the customers of El Morocco. I never heard of Bing ever doing that anyplace else."

The most widely publicized of all the Gleason gags was the time he bet Toots ten bucks that he could beat him in a race around the blocks on Fifty-first and Fifty-second streets. Gleason weighed 280 pounds at the time, and Toots couldn't put his ten bucks on the bar fast enough. Once again, the pigeon in Toots surfaced; Jackie conned him into running the race in opposite directions. And when Toots, almost purple, staggered into his saloon, there was Gleason already spending the ten bucks to buy himself a drink plus tip. Toots didn't know that Gleason had run a few steps away from Toots in the opposite direction and then hailed a cab until he read it in Bob Considine's column in the New York *Journal-American*.

Considine was a general news columnist for Hearst. He and Gleason were always arguing in Toots' about UFOs. Gleason believes in these strange lights from another planet. Considine never did—until one day.

"There would be these little lights," says Jackie, "traveling at great speeds around our aircraft in World War Two. We thought they were something the Germans had come up with. The Germans thought they were an Allied

Left: A rare photo of Jackie with his father, in the summer of 1925. On December 15 of that same year, Herb Gleason would vanish forever from the life of a little boy who loved his father very much. Sadly, Jackie says he has no pictures of his mother, Mae Kelly Gleason.

Below: The future star, at PS 73 in Brooklyn, knows that you always get yourself in center camera. It's no trouble picking him out in this photo, taken about the time Jackie made his show business debut as the emcee of the eighth-grade graduation show.

Facing page: In 1936, at the Club Miami in Newark, Jackie was knocking them dead onstage—and sometimes in the alley.

Above: Gleason's pal Tony Amico, new bride Gen Halford, and Gleason in front of a billboard in 1936. "Jumping Jackie Gleason"?

Below: Notice that Gleason is the only one without a drink in his hand at this party at Pat O'Brien's house that Flo and Jack Haley took him to in 1941. That's a young Bob Hope, just making it in radio, on the right. Left to right: Jackie, Flo, Jack, advertising executive Danny Danker, Lorena Danker, who later married Louis B. Mayer, Hope and wife Dolores.

Left: How can a guy who looks like Robert Taylor be so funny?

Below: A sketch from "Laughs Only" at Slapsy Maxie's in Hollywood, circa 1941. The girl is Lois Andrews, who became famous a few years earlier as George Jessel's fourteen-year-old bride, and the waiter is Bert Wheeler of the famous Wheeler and Woolsey comedy team of Broadway and the early talkies ("Rio Rita").

Right: Jackie Gleason, who was one handsome devil at this weight. Some Hollywood producers thought he should have been a leading man instead of a comedian. They may have been right.

Below: Jackie Gleason finally gets his name on the marquee of a Loew's State, only this one is in Pittsburgh, when Gleason took his Dumont show on the road just before the switch to CBS-TV in 1952.

Facing page: Jackie in a CBS-TV publicity still, circa 1955.

Right: You know this is an early photo of Jackie Gleason in his famous "And away we go!" move because he doesn't fill out his size 51 suit.

Above: George Jessel and Jackie at a Friars Roast in the fifties. Jessel was the perennial emcee at all Friars stages, both in New York and Hollywood.

Right: Jackie with broken leg he suffered on January 30, 1954, when he slipped onstage in a puddle of water during a silent movie spoof. Leonard Stern, one of the writers on the show, recalls that Jackie wrote this skit entirely by himself.

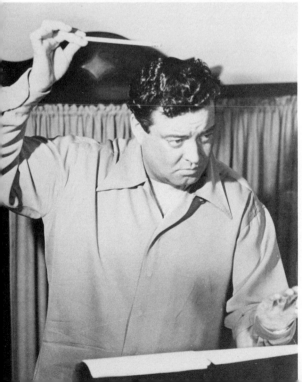

Above: That's Paul Whiteman, the King of Jazz, listening to Gleason do his famous trumpet bit. Jackie always did his trumpet routine with a real horn man behind the curtain.

Left: Jackie conducts a sixty-piece orchestra—with forty Italian mandolin pickers—for one of his top-selling albums.

Henny Youngman, the king of the one-liners, and Gleason mull over a gag
during a Miami Beach rehearsal in the sixties.

The maestro—who can't read a note of music—conducts his orchestra.
Trumpet star Bobby Hackett, who should know, once said Jackie knew what
he was doing musically at all times.

Left: Hustlers two. Gleason and billiards champion Willy Mosconi play some exhibition pool.

Facing page: The Great One as painted in oil.

Right: This is Jackie in 1961 on the second week of "You're in the Picture," one of the great disasters in television history. It was a prime-time game show that somebody at CBS-TV thought was terrific. This picture shows Jackie apologizing for the first show. Amazingly, his apology was so hilarious that it has become a classic example of how a great comedian can recover from a flop.

Above: Jackie and the Dorsey Brothers. That's Jimmy on the left and Tommy on the right. This is one of the few pictures showing the battling brothers smiling at each other.

Facing page, top: Three great bandleaders. Jackie with the late Count Basie and Guy Lombardo, two of the all-time greats in the big band era.

Facing page, bottom: Glynis Johns, Laurel Goodwin, and Jackie in 1962 in *Papa's Delicate Condition,* the story of silent star Corinne Griffith's tipsy father.

Jackie and his new Alice, Sue Ane Langdon, with midget Billy Curtis—just before the balloons almost carried him off—at Union Station, Los Angeles, before the Great Gleason Express took off for a ten-day trip cross-country in 1962.

Jackie and author James Bacon laughing it up as the Great Gleason Express rolls over the Mojave Desert in 1962. What a fun trip that was.

Gleason and child actress Katherine Kath in *Gigot*, a poignant tale of a deaf mute and a little girl in Paris. Made in 1962.

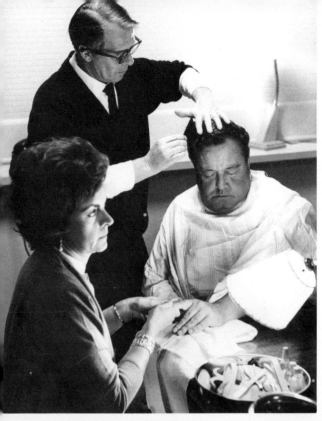

Left: Cary Grant once called Jackie the most stylish man in show business. This interlude in his dressing room helps tell you why.

Below: The one and only Toots Shor cutting up with his drinking buddy. That's famous Broadway columnist Earl Wilson looking o

invention. Considine and I were having a hell of an argument about this one day. I told him that four presidents of the United States had told me about these UFOs and no one knew what the hell they were. General Rosie O'Donnell, then head of our Strategic Air Force, overheard us and said to Bob, 'Jackie's right.' That's all he said and it shook up Considine."

Humphrey Bogart, Jackie's co-star in *All Through the Night,* a Warners classic, also drank with Jackie in Toots'. On St. Patrick's Day in 1952, Bogie talked Gleason into finishing up over at P. J. Clarke's, which Bogie knew would be filled with most of the Irishmen who'd marched in the parade. Now Bogie, in his time, started a thousand fights— but he never swung a punch in any of them himself. He was a notorious troublemaker.

As soon as they reached the bar at P. J. Clarke's, Bogie started talking loudly, saying that Saint Patrick was a no-good bum and he couldn't see why all the drunks in the place were celebrating his birthday.

"It's all a crock of shit," Bogie kept yelling. Minutes later a big Irishman grabbed Bogie by the coat lapels and told him matter-of-factly, "I know you're a movie tough guy and you don't have your stuntmen with you, but if you don't knock off this shit, I'm going to separate you from some of your capped teeth."

Bogart quivered his lip and then pointed to Gleason sipping his drink at the bar. "Not with my friend here, you don't," said Bogie. At that, Gleason grabbed Bogie and they went back to Toots', where peace always reigned.

· 10 ·
POW!
ALICE,
RIGHT
ON
THE
KISSER!

With Pert Kelton gone, Jackie's most pressing business was finding a new Alice before he could make his debut on CBS-TV in the fall of 1952.

Jackie and Bullets Durgom auditioned dozens of actresses but couldn't come up with the right girl to replace Pert, who, in three seasons, had put her own trademark on the part. Then one day Bullets ran into Val Irving, who is still the manager of Audrey Meadows. Val was on his way to Audrey's apartment, and Bullets went along to see if Audrey knew of an actress who could play Alice Kramden. Audrey herself was starring at the time in a hit Broadway musical, *Top Banana,* with Phil Silvers. Audrey recalls how she got the job:

□

"Every actress I named Jackie had already seen and rejected. Then, out of the blue, I said, 'I know a girl who is absolutely perfect for this part.' Both Val and Bullets asked 'Who?' at the same time. I answered, 'Me.'

"The next day Val and Bullets took me over to see Jackie, who was nice as can be, but he asked me to wait outside his office in that big penthouse at the Park Sheraton. He was in the midst of doing a big layout for *Life* magazine and said he would discuss me with Val and Bullets. Fine.

"Later I heard from Val that Jackie jumped all over the two men, saying, 'Have you guys got needles in your heads? This girl is too young and pretty to play Alice. She could never be an Irish housewife in a Brooklyn tenement.'

"When I heard that, I really went after the part seriously. I knew that *Top Banana* was going on the road and I wanted to stay in New York. When I first went over to see Jackie, I had honestly felt that it was more or less a joke. Now I wanted that part. I told Val to get a photographer over to my place early the next morning. I promised him I wouldn't get out of bed until the photographer showed up. I fixed my hair in some unglamorous hairdo and wore no makeup. I put on an old, sloppy dress and we shot the pictures. I knew they were down to the wire, looking for a new Alice, so we had the pictures developed that same day."

Bullets took the pictures over to Gleason and threw them in front of him. There was no name attached. As Bullets recalls:

"Gleason looks at the pictures and yells at the top of his voice, 'That's our Alice! Who is she?'

"I said, 'You bastard! that's the same redhead you said was too young and pretty the other day. That's Audrey

Meadows.' Gleason laughed and said, 'Well, anyone with that sense of humor deserves the part.'"

And so, Jackie signed his new Alice, one who would produce great comic chemistry with The Great One. She drove a hard bargain, though—two of her brothers were lawyers (one of them later became a judge).

"My brothers and my lawyer from the union (AFTRA) faced the nine lawyers that Jackie and CBS brought up from Washington. My lawyers asked for residuals in perpetuity and got them." Standard payment for residuals is normally limited to five reruns which, for most shows, is generous. But "The Honeymooners" was not a normal show. Audrey says Jackie recently asked her: "How did you ever pull that off?"

Audrey says it was easy because no one ever figured back in 1952 that "The Honeymooners" would still be running more than thirty years later. Art Carney and Joyce Randolph took the standard contract and were cut off at five reruns years ago.

"Do you know," says Audrey, "that 'The Honeymooners' is the longest-running situation comedy in television history, even running longer than 'I Love Lucy?'" Audrey also is the longest-running residual-collector in television history; she should be in the Guinness Book of World Records.

Audrey had no problem getting out of her contract with *Top Banana*. Phil Silvers even arranged for her to beat the standard two-week Equity notice. She recalls her first "Honeymooners" sketch:

"I came out of the theater, where everybody is re-hearsal-happy. Even Phil loved to rehearse. Everybody does but Jackie. We had a read-through of the script, and all week I kept wondering where Jackie was. Finally, when

it came close to airtime, I asked Art, 'When do we rehearse?' Art answered, 'Do you remember that first read-
through? That was all the rehearsal you'll get.'

"And it was. In that very first show, I got a baptism by
fire. Ralph came home screaming, 'You're not going to
serve me frozen steak again?' He picked up the steak,
which wasn't steak but a piece of wood painted like a steak.
It was the first time any of us had seen this prop. Jackie
slammed the phony steak on the table as only he could
slam. It broke in two pieces and one of them flew out into
the audience. Now it's live going out to fifty million people.
And Jackie is staring at me, wondering how the new girl is
going to handle this unexpected development. I picked up
the one half of the wooden steak that stayed on the table
and said, 'No, Ralph. I'm not serving you frozen steak
again. I'm serving you half a frozen steak.'

"Then I walked over to the door and it wouldn't open.
I ad-libbed, 'Ralph, I told you to get this door fixed.' Then
I pulled again and this time it opened. The people up in the
control booth were going nuts trying to find those lines in
the script. My first two lines in my first episode, and both
were ad-libbed. Maybe that's why Jackie didn't want to rehearse."

Jackie had found his perfect Alice. Here was a girl
who could cope with crisis. But Audrey recalls that she was
in tears when she went to her dressing room:

"The next week, I told Jackie, 'You may not like to
rehearse, but the rest of us do. We are going to rehearse
and we will leave a blank spot on the floor and that blank
spot will be you. So when we go on the air Saturday night,
you just get in your blank spots and say whatever you
want.'

"You know, he didn't raise any objections. I love that
man.

□

"And I think it's a disgrace that both Art Carney and I won Emmys and Jackie Gleason hasn't got one."

Audrey will always be the definitive Alice, because the episodes she was in were the ones that were filmed. But it was not always that easy. Her sister Jayne Meadows Allen recalls: "The first couple of years Audrey did Alice live. She used to come home crying that Jackie didn't appreciate her as much as he did Pert; that he didn't give her the funny lines that Pert had."

At about the same time that Gleason made Audrey Meadows his Alice Kramden, he hired his old crap-shooting pal from Las Vegas to write for the Gleason show. That was Leonard Stern, who is now one third of the Los Angeles publishing house of Price, Stern and Sloan, but was always noted for his comedy writing. He was a writer for "The Jackie Gleason Show" and Phil Silvers' "Sergeant Bilko" in the fifties—and those are just about the Rolls-Royces of comedy.

"I came back east and I had watched the Gleason show in Hollywood. You could see that 'The Honeymooners,' which was only a ten-minute sketch, dominated the show. I have the distinction of writing the first long 'Honeymooners' show, the first conscious effort to build the whole show around Alice and Ralph Kramden.

"Jackie had only hired me for a four-week tryout and I asked for four thousand a week, a lot of money, but I needed that much to keep my place in Hollywood and pay for all my expenses in New York.

"I no sooner got in town than Jackie called me on the phone. 'Leonard,' he said, 'we're old friends. That four thousand a week is outrageous.' He was at CBS by this time and I told him that I really needed that much. I had to have it.

☐

"'Okay,' he said, 'You've got it but we're not friends anymore.'"

As Jackie got more popular on national television, his stock at home took a nosedive. He and Gen had split up, and on December 15, 1952, Jackie wrote to the chancery of the archdiocese of New York about ending the marriage officially. Often, in those days, Catholics would consult the Church before they called lawyers, especially when seeking separate maintenance (a separation but not a divorce). After the chancery received Jackie's letter, that archdiocesan office got in touch with Gen, and before long, a Supreme Court justice of the state of New York legalized a decree of separate maintenance. In it, Jackie agreed to pay Gen 12½ percent of his earnings off the top. Additionally, the two girls would each get one per cent of the gross for their education. Ironically, Jackie's separation from his family, by bed and board, came on the exact date—December 15—that his own father had disappeared in 1925. It was not the greatest Christmas present any way you look at it.

Daughter Geraldine recalls: "We didn't see too much of Dad after the separate maintenance. When he did come over to see us, he might stay only a half hour or so. As kids, it hurt us some that we didn't have a full-time father. It doesn't hurt us now because as we got older, we realized that our father has a built-in shyness that won't allow him to get close to anyone, not even those he loves.

"A lot of people put him down for that. Linda and I did too, for years, but no more. That is just the way he is. We know now that he always loved us but had a hard time showing affection. Sometimes he would express that love in lavish gifts. We never wanted for anything in all our lives. My dad is extremely generous."

□

Geraldine can't bear to watch her father on television when he does The Poor Soul, his great sad-faced clown character.

"That character is much too sad for me. I think that lost look on his face mirrors all that tragedy he had as a young boy growing up in Brooklyn. He got such a rotten deal in his early life that it made him unable to give of himself. We are very close today with Dad because we know how he is; that no one or nothing will ever change him."

Through the winter of 1953, Jackie couldn't be accused of any philandering; he was legally separated and a free-swinging bachelor. And yet, the final parting from Gen after sixteen years was tough on Jackie, and even tougher on Gen. Jackie knew that it was the odd-couple aspect of his marriage that caused its disintegration. But when he tired of the one-night stands with the showgirls and party girls, he again, late in 1953, went for the same kind of girl as Gen. Pure, wholesome, a devout Catholic, pretty. She had joined the June Taylor dancers while still a teenager because she had an older sister to look after her. Her name was Marilyn Taylor and, like Gen, she was a ballerina. Bullets Durgom recalls:

"I remember telling Jackie, 'There's a girl who has class.' She was not hard-boiled like many of the other showgirls around town. She was different, and before long, Jackie was pursuing Marilyn."

Marilyn was reluctant at first to date Jackie. As one of the dancers on the show, she had met Gen and Jackie's daughters before the separation. Jackie was legally separated when he went after Marilyn, but a romance with him didn't jibe with the moral character and religious views of a good Catholic girl.

But she was young and vulnerable and she found out,

□

like many a girl had before her, that it was hard to with-
stand the Gleason charm. Eventually, the twenty-eight-
year-old Marilyn fell for Jackie, and he already had fallen
hard for her. They were in love.

In olden days, lovers wrote poetry for the women they
loved. Jackie Gleason, who couldn't read a note of music,
composed songs for Marilyn. Tender love songs. He had
always been a frustrated musician and had been fascinated
with sounds ever since his mother kept him cooped up in
that Brooklyn tenement. But how could a guy who couldn't
read music compose it?

Bobby Hackett, the great trumpet virtuoso with whom
Jackie became friendly during the making of *Orchestra
Wives* with the Glenn Miller band, once gave this expert
opinion:

"Jackie knows a lot more about music than he is given
credit for. I have seen him conduct a sixty-piece orchestra
and detect one discordant note in the brass section. He
would immediately stop the music and locate the wrong
note. It always amazed the professional musicians how a
guy who technically didn't know one note from another
could do that. And he was never wrong."

The lovesick comedian sat at the piano one day in
March of 1953 with a professional arranger by the name of
Pete King who wrote down the one-fingered melodies the
comedian had in his head. The result was two songs—
"Lovers' Rhapsody" and "Melancholy Serenade," which
would become the haunting theme of "The Jackie Gleason
Show."

When you are Jackie Gleason and you have written
two love songs for the woman you love, where do you go
next? An album, of course. In 1953, albums were not that
big in the recording business. The 45-RPM singles were the
hot stuff, and the kids were all playing a rhythm and blues

□

song called "One Mint Julep." The rock 'n' roll revolution was coming down the pike. One would have thought that recording companies would have jumped to get television's hottest comedian on their label, but no way. Who wanted a comedian conducting a big orchestra in an album of romantic melodies? The rhythm and blues beat was on.

True, David Rose, composer of "Holiday for Strings," was doing pretty well with his romantic albums. So was Paul Weston, once an arranger for Tommy Dorsey, with romantic albums that often featured his wife, Jo Stafford.

Rose recalls being awakened, sometimes as early as 2 A.M., in his Sherman Oaks, California, home only to listen to his own albums being played over the telephone. "This went on for a week or so. It was driving me nuts because no one would answer me. Only my own albums could be heard. Finally, one morning came the voice of Jackie Gleason. He said, 'We've been sitting around all week playing your albums. They're great.'"

None of the recording studios wanted to make an album with Jackie, so he made his own, renting a studio at Decca. Even though Jackie had signed an $11 million contract with CBS, he still had to borrow money to make the album. You had to be around Jackie in those days. He believed money was something one threw from the backs of trains. He made Diamond Jim Brady look like a skinflint.

Bullets Durgom, who knew something about music from all his years with the Tommy Dorsey and Glenn Miller bands, lent Jackie four thousand dollars. Then Bullets and Jackie got into a big argument and Bullets took back his four thousand.

"It was the most expensive hassle of my life," Bullets recalls. "I think my share of that first album would have come to about one hundred thousand dollars."

For that first album, Jackie picked all the songs he

□

119

liked to drink by at 2 A.M.—"I'm in the Mood for Love," "I Only Have Eyes for You," and "My Funny Valentine." The album was called "For Lovers Only." Gleason hired a sixty-piece orchestra that he conducted, and he did such unique things as using forty Italian mandolin players, who were told to dip their picks in water. Bobby Hackett was the sole trumpet player.

"With all those Italian mandolin pickers, you couldn't get a haircut in New York within a forty-mile radius," says Jackie.

Decca wanted no part of the finished album. Neither did any of the other labels. Finally, Bullets got a measly one-thousand-dollar advance from Capitol in return for a promise of some free publicity on "The Jackie Gleason Show" on CBS-TV.

No one at Capitol dreamed what that television publicity would do for record sales. *For Lovers Only* sold a phenomenal half a million copies. After that, all the record companies were after Gleason, but he stayed with Capitol, the only label who would have him for the first album.

As David Rose comments: "The SOB put me out of business."

Jackie, with his keen sense of what the public wanted, had reasoned that half of the world was in love, as he was with Marilyn, and the other half was torching for a lost love. Most of the albums that followed in rapid succession had romantic titles, such as *Music to Remember, Music, Martinis and Memories, Music to Make You Misty,* and *Melancholy Serenade,* which featured his own compositions. There was also one with more of a beat to it, called *Awaay We Go!*

The albums dominated the record charts for months, each of them selling over a million copies. Gleason the comedian all of a sudden became the new André Kostelanetz, who also had sold millions of records featuring soft strings and romantic melodies.

After the success of the albums, Jackie, to everybody's surprise, composed music for a television ballet called *Tawny,* a four-part symphonic tone poem. Before this, everybody had figured Jackie's musical background to be strictly Dixieland and the big band sounds of his drinking pals, the Dorsey brothers. But in the fall of 1953 he conceived what then would be the biggest production number in the history of television—a complete ballet. The network brass thought he was crazy; a ballet was considered to be too much for the little screen to handle—it would get lost outside of the Metropolitan Opera stage or the Cinemascope movie screen. The folks at CBS, executives and technicians alike, told him that it would be impossible to stage. Of course, that only made Jackie think in more grandiose terms; it was his show, and he was going to do the ballet.

Before rehearsing the ballet, choreographed by June Taylor, Jackie got his show conductor, Ray Bloch, to assemble a fifty-five-piece symphony orchestra. Jackie conducted this orchestra himself and, waving the baton like Toscanini, rehearsed this group for several hours. And then, for an hour more, while the union musicians waited, at $27.50 each per hour, Jackie worked with the sound mixers. Then he held them over for another hour on golden time—double the $27.50 scale—while he listened to the playback. It cost Gleason roughly $10,000.

Jackie, now getting his big paychecks from CBS-TV, paid for everything out of his own pocket, but this session was not for an album. It was just for a playback recording for June Taylor to use while rehearsing her seventy-six dancers.

When it came time to put *Tawny* on live before mil-

□

lions of people, Gleason had fifty musicians and seventy-six dancers onstage at the same time. In that era of black-and-white television, many people in the United States were still watching on twelve-inch screens, and to counteract this, Gleason wanted the show shot with five cameras. No television show, up to that time, had ever used that many cameras. Gleason wanted the fifth camera high on a balcony, for a Busby Berkeley effect on the dancers below. He wanted this camera with a zoom lens. CBS technicians threw up their hands, but Gleason got everything he wanted.

Came show time and the ballet lasted an incredible twenty minutes on the tube. The CBS technicians admitted that Gleason had taught them something new about their craft. The network brass was also impressed, even though the ballet cost a whopping $30,000. CBS-TV wasn't too worried abut the cost because Gleason's contract provided him with $120,000 a week for thirty-nine weeks to deliver a variety show each Saturday night, which included the cost of airtime on the CBS network. Since jackie gleason enterprises owned the show, it meant that the cost of the ballet came out of Gleason's pocket. If the weekly budget exceeded $120,000, it was Gleason's loss, not the network's.

The real icing on the cake came from the critics. Jack Gould, *The New York Times* television columnist, was the most powerful critic in the nation, and he was also rated one of the toughest. He wrote: "Bravo for Jackie Gleason. One of the most exciting hits of the video season . . . a poem for eye and ear . . . money well spent."

And *Variety,* the show-business bible, said: "Last Saturday, it was composer Gleason's moment."

Tawny was not the Bolshoi, but it certainly was superior television entertainment. Capitol immediately grabbed the sound track, which Gleason had made just for a rehearsal playback, and distributed it as an album. It sold more than a million copies. The great conductor Percy Faith wrote Jackie a fan letter in which he asked: "If you can't read music, how can you compose and conduct like you do?"

Gleason wrote back: "Well, if you write a story, you don't need a typewriter. Shakespeare didn't have one."

Hugo Winterhalter, another famed conductor, wired Jackie this terse message: "Fuck Juilliard." Jimmy Petrillo, head of the American Federation of Musicians, sent Jackie an honorary gold card, so that he could conduct union musicians anytime and anyplace. Even the prestigious Metropolitan Opera offered Gleason the role of the jailer in *Die Fledermaus,* which he turned down although opera is the only thing Jackie hasn't done in showbusiness.

Jackie, in retrospect, says, "The way I did my music was a very simple idea. If I had been a professional musician, I probably wouldn't have put Hackett and his trumpet with forty mandolins, yet it gave the album a romantic touch that was totally unique. People love romance."

Marilyn loved her new musical boyfriend. What girl wouldn't appreciate a lover who composed love songs for her, songs that a whole nation was buying in the millions? Their romance, however, had a few pitfalls to overcome. The worst came after the night—January 30, 1954—when Jackie broke his leg on camera. He had slipped in a puddle of water onstage during a satire of a silent movie. Art Carney had to close the show for the injured star.

Ironically, the show had one of the biggest ratings ever. The show was taped live in New York but delayed for West Coast prime-time viewing due to the three-hour time difference. "Everybody in the East was telephoning their relatives and friends in California to watch the Gleason show. Jackie broke his leg on camera. How do you like

□

123

that? A broken leg gets you a better Nielsen rating than a good show," comments Jackie.

Jackie was taken to Doctor's Hospital from the Hammerstein Theater, now a CBS studio. Before long, his hospital room looked like his penthouse—plenty of food and booze. There also was a big television set. One afternoon, he and Marilyn were watching television when Gen suddenly showed up. Although separated from her Jackie, she was concerned about her ex-husband's accident.

When Gen found Marilyn there, she started hitting on Jackie and then on Marilyn, who avoided all argument by staring straight ahead at the television set. She hadn't been the other woman—there was no other woman when Jackie and Gen officially ended their marriage thirteen months earlier—and Marilyn didn't want to be cast in that position. What the hell kind of a predicament was this? At the urging of Jackie's doctor, Gen left the room. A nurse leaked the confrontation to columnist Jack O'Brian, then writing for the New York *Journal-American*. This infuriated Gleason, and when, after his recovery, he saw O'Brian in Toots Shor's, he stormed: "Don't you ever write about my wife and girlfriend again." Then he asked O'Brian to return the expensive watch Gleason had given the columnist for a Christmas present.

All that publicity about the confrontation in the hospital room turned Jackie's romance with Marilyn into a game of hide-and-seek, with all the secrecy of a CIA operation. It shouldn't have. Jackie and Gen had long been split, but such are the peculiarities of Irish behavior. While an Irishman may often get drunk and fall down in public, he considers the only shame to be when someone whispers about his home life. And Jackie knew that he had been the scoundrel in the breakup with Gen. That's what hurt the most.

□

The romance between Jackie and Marilyn continued, however secretly. In the summer of 1954, during a hiatus from the television show, Jackie wanted to take Marilyn to Europe. They did not go together. Jackie took one flight; Marilyn left the next day in the company of Tony Amico, Jackie's buddy from the old Club Miami days and Mother Mutzenbacher's.

Marilyn wanted to do the usual tourist bit—see the churches and museums. She saw little but airports and hotel suites. The day Jackie hit a major European capital, he wanted to leave on the next available flight. He thought that the Italian food in Italy was lousy, and that it was much better in New York. The trio only spent three hours in Paris, waiting for a boat train to take them to London.

Finally, in London, Jackie settled down for a stay. People knew him there. He spoke the language and there were lots of parties. They stayed a week or two.

Going back, the trio (Jackie, Marilyn, and Tony) booked passage on the luxury liner *United States*. Lou Walters, an old nightclub boss of Jackie's, was also a passenger, so Jackie had someone to talk show business with.

When they returned to New York, Jackie decided that there would be thirty-two dancers in June Taylor's group, instead of the previous sixteen. Marilyn had been one of the sixteen, and she was now one of the thirty-two. Jackie Gleason was the star of the show. Marilyn wanted to get married. She knew it was hopeless, but what can a girl who is in love with an overweight comedian do?

· 11 ·
THE HONEYMOON'S NOT OVER FOR GLEASON

In 1955, the Brooklyn Dodgers beat the New York Yankees in the World Series, and "The Honeymooners" was filmed. What a great year for Brooklyn.

In a sense, "The Honeymooners" was television's first spin-off. When it first went on the air in 1951 on the old Dumont Network, it was just a sketch on "The Cavalcade of Stars," one of many sketches. Obviously, it was the most popular. Mail for that sketch was measured by sacks, not bundles.

And as good as Pert Kelton was in the original sketches, it soon became evident that Ralph Kramden had found the perfect Alice in Audrey Meadows. Born in China, the daughter of an Episcopal missionary, she was

□

such a good actress that she became as authentic a part of that little Brooklyn kitchen as the pan under the dripping icebox.

Meadows and Carney, along with Joyce Randolph—the new and definitive Trixie—would have liked more rehearsal with their star, but they both knew that, to Gleason, rehearsal was a four-letter word. So the trio didn't complain. They rehearsed among themselves, and when the show went on the air in 1955, filmed full-speed ahead, before a live audience, all three played it Gleason's way.

Audrey recalls that Jackie's control of his show was so potent, he even used to edit "The Honeymooners" while the show was going out live to millions of people, or when it was filmed in one take before a live audience.

"Jackie had an uncanny sense of timing. In fact, I used to think he had a time clock in his head. He knew instinctively when a show was playing too long. When that happened, he would come up with a line that was two pages ahead of what we were doing at the moment. Art and I rolled with this but I have seen veteran actors in the show who were near collapse after it happened. He could drop two minutes without even the slightest hint, not even a wink. And, amazingly, he always cut without hurting the plot in any way.

"Jackie was not the easiest person in the world to act with, but he certainly was the most fun. I remember once or twice when he would forget his own lines. It's a wonder it didn't happen more often, since he was doing everything on the show, acting, directing, helping with the choreography and the music, plus most of the production work.

"One particular incident I remember vividly. The script had Jackie telling me about a new theory he had for dealing with wives. I was peeling potatoes at the time and then I saw Jackie just walking around. I couldn't give the plot away, so I said, 'Okay, Ralph. Tell me about it. I just know it's time for another theory on how to deal with wives.' I gave him my usual disgusted look and he picked up right away. 'Very funny, Alice. It just so happens, I do have a theory on how to deal with wives.'"

Audrey recalls that she usually wore aprons on the show, and fans used to send her aprons by the dozens. They would also send curtains, because the Kramden flat had no curtains on the window.

The decision to film, instead of doing it live on the air, came about in one of those ruthless ways for which television always has been noted. Mike Kirk, who represented the advertising agency for Buick, visited the Gleason office in the summer of 1955. He had an idea: Why not put the live sketch on film as a weekly half-hour situation comedy, with Buick as the sponsor? Everybody on the Gleason show loved the idea of filming "The Honeymooners." There was only one problem. Milton Berle's show, now sponsored by Buick instead of Texaco, was number two in the ratings on Tuesday night. (Believe it or not, Gleason's old friend, now on Dumont television delivering sermons, was number one—Bishop Fulton J. Sheen. "Bishop Sheen had better writers than I. He had Mark, Luke and John working for him. For a while, we had the same sponsor— Sky Chief," says Milton.) And so, the first thing Jackie wanted to know of Kirk was, would he be overthrowing Berle, who was Mr. Television?

Well, it happened with no apologies or reasons given. In the fall of 1955, Uncle Miltie found himself without a Buick in his garage, and NBC-TV lost one of its biggest sponsors to rival CBS-TV. (Berle was not bitter about losing Buick to Gleason. He knows how cruel the business can be.)

□

That first year on film, "The Honeymooners" had a flock of writers whom Gleason seldom saw. Usually, they slid the scripts under Gleason's door. The head writers were Walter Stone and the late Marvin Marx; they did many of "The Honeymooners" episodes that are still being shown today. Harry Crane had hired Stone and Marx as kids, and they were damn good. Crane himself had left the Gleason show when Dean Martin and Jerry Lewis offered him as much money to do six shows a year as the Gleason show paid for thirty-nine. It was an offer he couldn't refuse, for although he was a native of Brooklyn, Harry didn't like living in New York, and besides the money, Martin and Lewis meant California sunshine.

Before leaving for the West Coast, Harry went over to Doctor's Hospital to say good-bye to Gleason.

"He was in the hospital for losing weight. Anyhow, when I go to his room to say good-bye, he's not there. I asked the nurse, 'Where's Jackie?' 'Oh,' she said. 'He said he wasn't feeling well, so he went home.'"

This was not an unusual thing with Jackie. When he first joined the show after Crane had left, Leonard Stern wanted to see Jackie.

"Jack Philbin said he was unavailable. I told Jack that Jackie and I were old friends and that I wanted to see him. He was in Doctors Hospital, either losing weight or getting over a hangover. I went over there and the nurse told me the same thing—'Mr. Gleason is not well so he went home.' I know the story has been around but it actually happened."

In 1955, with the show on film, there weren't even re-rehearsals for the cameras. Jackie remembers:
"Once our cameraman said he absolutely needed a re-

□

hearsal. I told him: 'Just have the damn camera follow me.' Where the hell am I going to go? Out the door?''

Jackie could be a tough taskmaster when it got near airtime. All great producers are, or else the crew and cast would trample them to death. If a member of the cast or crew did what they were supposed to, they never heard from Jackie. But if they shirked, all hell could break loose with The Great One.

Bullets Durgom recalls that Jackie even concerned himself with business affairs but as Bullets says, "Lee Iacocca he was not."

The best example of this is that, after the first thirty-nine episodes of "The Honeymooners" had been filmed in 1955–56, Jackie refused to film the second year. That's why television buffs have kept watching those same thirty-nine shows year after year, from 1955 to the present.

"Everybody thought I was nuts turning down seven million bucks to film that second year of my contract. [Jackie's Buick contract was $14 million for two years.] I know CBS and Buick thought I had gotten a better offer someplace else. They offered me more money but I turned it down. They wouldn't believe me when I said we couldn't come up with the same high quality of scripts that second year. It was that simple."

One of the fringe benefits of Jackie's deal with CBS, along with the free home in Peekskill and a guarantee of $100,000 per year for fifteen years, in exchange for Jackie's working exclusively for CBS, was that Jackie retained complete ownership of the filmed "Honeymooners." But, to everyone's surprise, Jackie sold out his ownership rights in 1957 to MCA, Ltd., for a paltry $2 million, which is nothing compared to what those shows have earned in syndication for the last thirty years. (Just to compare, "Gilligan's

Island," which began a decade later, has already passed the billion-dollar mark in syndication sales.)

Bullets Durgom estimates that Jackie lost a cool $100 million by selling out. And Bullets himself lost another $15 million in commissions.

"I knew what I was doing," says Jackie now. "Hell, if I still owned those thirty-nine shows, I would need a small army of people to keep track of them. I'm not cut out to be a tycoon."

(In 1985, however, Jackie became a tycoon when seventy-five taped sketches of "The Honeymooners" were taken out of the vault and edited, first for a season on the Showtime cable network, and second, in 1986, for release to commercial station syndication. Jackie is a partner with Viacom in the new enterprise, and it was Viacom that syndicated the thirty-nine filmed episodes all those years under the MCA license.)

No matter how famous Jackie got on television, he never became too famous for his old friends. True, some of the guys from the old neighborhood were reluctant to approach him after he'd become a big star. They needn't have been. Whenever Julia Dennehey Marshall came to his show, Gleason put out the red carpet for her. It was the same with old school chum Thomas ("Bookshelf") Robinson, who became vice president of Pace University in New York. Some, like boyhood chum Teddy Gilanza and Pop Dennehey, became regulars in the Joe the Bartender sketches, which was based on Jimmy Proce's saloon in the old Bushwick neighborhood. ("Bookshelf" Robinson, as his nickname tabs him, is believed to be the only high school graduate, certainly the only college graduate, who was in Jackie's street gang—the Nomads.)

The Nomads were not the violent kind of gang that prowl Brooklyn streets today. When they got together, it

□

was mostly to talk about girls, smoke Camels, which you could buy three for a penny in those days, and drink Dago Red, the homemade Prohibition wine that Teddy's father made in the cellar of his tenement.

And Pop Dennehey lived long enough to sit in front of his television set in Brooklyn and hear Joe the Bartender ask, "What'll you have, Mr. Dennehey?" He still couldn't understand how Jackie, the well-dressed pool hustler of the neighborhood, became such a big television star.

Another neighbor was Sadie Youngman, who lived at 410 Chauncey Street, a few doors from Jackie's place. That's where she and her comedian husband of more than fifty-five years first met. Little did she know then that she would become Henny Youngman's most famous one-liner—"Take my wife. Please!" And little did she know that her neighbor would become the great star that he did.

And Gleason always made sure that some part was written into a sketch for Sammy Birch, his pal from the Halsey Theater days.

Gleason often returned to the old neighborhood, usually in a limousine. First stop would always be Jimmy Proce's saloon, where he would buy a few rounds for his old gang. Harry Crane recalls the time they saw a guy get out of a cab to hock a piece of jewelry in a pawnshop.

"Only in Bushwick," said Jackie, "would you ever see a guy take a cab to a hockshop. No wonder I have such expensive tastes."

The romance with Marilyn continued as fiercely as ever, though it still was a no-win situation for them both. Gen was adamant that she would never give Jackie the divorce he wanted. Jackie wanted to marry Marilyn, but what grounds could he have used against Gen? She was not at fault in the separate-maintenance decree, which legally

□

meant that Jackie and Gen were separated only by domiciles, and that they were not free to remarry. And the last thing CBS-TV wanted with typical network morality was divorce headlines for its biggest comedian. (The network also objected to Jackie's drinking, not realizing that it was part of his appeal with millions of viewers.)

"The Honeymooners" was no longer filmed, but it was back on "The Jackie Gleason Show" in 1956 as a live sketch. All the other Gleason characters were there too, including the one and only Reggie Van Gleason the Third.

Perhaps the funniest Reggie sketch in 1956 was the one in which the network arranged for its all-time top newsman, Edward R. Murrow, to bring his popular "Person to Person" show to interview Reggie. The sketch had the Park Avenue playboy, dressed in white tie and tails, in the living room of his penthouse apartment, standing regally before a model train display that must have had hobbyists across the nation drooling. As Murrow, from a remote studio per his usual custom, asked Reggie about his life-style in the familiar Murrow delivery, a model freight train carrying a single shot glass of whiskey over miniature bridges and through toy tunnels stopped before The Great One. Gleason lifted the shot glass as Murrow asked, "Are model trains your hobby, Reggie?"

"No, booze," said Reggie, downing the whiskey in one fast gulp.

(Gleason's decision not to film "The Honeymooners" for that second season for 1956–57 was hard on his old network. He had been the best customer of Dumont's Electronicam, the three-camera setup that permitted the filming of a live show. If Dumont had not come up with the process, the Gleason show would have had to move to Hollywood to film "The Honeymooners." And now Elec-

tronicam, the only such filming process in New York, was
without a major client.)

In 1956, the Gleason format was the same as it had
been during the filming in the previous year. All the regulars were in the first half of the show: the June Taylor
dancers, the poster girls, and all the skits with Reggie, The
Poor Soul, Joe the Bartender and Stanley R. Sogg. Sogg
was the pitchman for the Late, Late, Late, Late, Late,
Late, Late Show who made outrageous offers to viewers,
such as one for a piece of wood stolen "from the front
porch of Huntz Hall" (one of the original Dead End kids.)
The movies on Sogg's show, of course, always starred "the
ever popular Mae Busch." And then "The Honeymooners," now a live sketch, closed the variety show.
Filmed or live, "The Honeymooners" was the most popular
sketch of the Gleason hour.

There was no other show like it on television. "I Love
Lucy" (CBS, 1951–57) was outrageous; "The Phil Silvers
Show" (CBS, 1955–59) was a riot that appealed to veterans
who had known a Sergeant Bilko in every outfit in World
War II; "The Bob Cummings Show" (NBC, CBS, NBC,
1955–59) was all about Cummings' sex life; and "Father
Knows Best" (CBS, NBC, CBS, 1954–60) had Robert
Young as superdaddy. "The Adventures of Ozzie and Har-
riet" (ABC, 1952–66) lasted for fourteen years, and a
whole generation grew up with a family whose father never
had a visible job "Make Room for Daddy" (ABC, CBS,
1953–64) lasted eleven years and made Danny Thomas the
first father on television who wasn't stupid.

All of these shows had one thing in common: they
were distinctively upper-middle-class. Even Bilko's bar-
racks were as middle-class as army life could be. In contrast
to all this competition, Gleason put his show into a

□

Brooklyn slum, peopled by a bus driver and his drab wife. Their kitchen set was so dreary that it didn't even have an electric refrigerator, which all the others had. Instead, the Kramden kitchen had an old-fashioned icebox, with a pan underneath it to catch the melting ice water.

And now we have an organization called RALPH, with more than 8,000 members who range from rock stars Bruce Springsteen and Cyndi Lauper to Don Baylor, the New York Yankees' slugger.

RALPH was founded by Bob Columbe and Peter Crescenti of Long Island University to keep "The Honeymooners" on the air. Members of RALPH can tell you what Ralph Kramden's social security number is—it's 105-36-22, which doesn't have the usual number of digits, but that only makes it funnier. They know that Ralph Kramden was born in Brooklyn but now drives a bus in Manhattan for the Gotham Bus Company and that his route is Madison Avenue. They know that before Ralph worked for the bus company, he delivered groceries for the A & P, and that he shoveled snow for the WPA during the Depression. They know that he had an uncle who wanted him to become an architect, but that Ralph gave it up to learn the Charleston. RALPH members, some of whom have seen each of the thirty-nine filmed episodes more than a hundred times, know of all this trivia about their favorite show—and scads more.

Not even "Lucy" has inspired such a cult. But why has "The Honeymooners" outlasted all of the other shows, with the exception of "Lucy"?

When Gleason created "The Honeymooners," he knew there were far more losers in the nation than winners. And for every loser, Gleason knew that a dreamer was locked up inside. Ralph Kramden is the biggest loser, and the biggest dreamer, in television history. He's Everyman, a fatso with thin ideas that never work.

Ralph comes up with ideas that can make him rich, such as no-cal pizza. The dreams are all impossible dreams, and everybody knows it—especially Alice, who deflates her balloon of a husband each week by saying, "Forget it, Ralph." And Ralph replies: "You don't love me, Alice. You just married me for my uniform." (The uniform happens to be a size 51 bus driver's uniform.)

Gleason's best pal works in the sewer, and his pal's wife is an ex-stripper. That's a little farfetched for Everyman, but somehow, with Art Carney and Joyce Randolph, it works.

In fact, the whole show works—and always has—because four of the best comedy actors in the business make it work. Jokes grow old but real-life characterizations never do. That's the secret of longevity: Emotions last longer than one-liners do.

The question Gleason is asked most often today is whether such a show as "The Honeymooners" could have been produced in today's television market. Says Jackie:

"Imagine going to a network executive and telling them you have an idea for a show that has a bus driver and his wife living in a Brooklyn slum and whose best friends are a sewer worker married to an ex-stripper?

"They would throw me out of the joint."

· 12 ·
GLEASON
DISCOVERS
ELVIS

It was Jackie Gleason, not Ed Sullivan, who first discovered Elvis Presley for television. Gleason did it in January, 1956, more than half a year before Ed featured Elvis on that controversial show which only focused on half of Elvis—from the waist up.

Ed Sullivan got all the page-one headlines, though, because of his moralistic stand against Elvis' pelvic movements, which many mothers said were exciting glands in girls too young to know what glands were. (Despite all his years as a Broadway columnist, Ed was a Puritan at heart.)

One more of the lucrative fringe benefits Gleason got from that $14 million contract with Buick and CBS-TV in 1955 was that he could produce his own summer replacement show, which was called "Stage Show." It starred the

□

battling Dorsey Brothers, Tommy and Jimmy, both drinking buddies of Gleason's from Toots Shor's saloon. And it was on "Stage Show" that Elvis made his national television debut.

Of course, the real discoverer of Elvis was his lifetime career manager, "Colonel" Tom Parker, who was a friend of Gleason's from Toots Shor's. Where else? The colorful Colonel, a former sideshow barker, had a carny act of dancing chickens. (The chickens actually danced because the Colonel made a hot plate look like a miniature stage.) Singer Gene ("My Blue Heaven") Austin admired such ingenuity, and made Parker his road manager. He and Austin were regulars at Toots' place.

In 1954, the Colonel took a hiatus from Austin and toured the Bible Belt of the Deep South with an old-fashioned medicine show, selling a tonic called Hadacol. It actually was a triple martini with vitamins. Within three months, sales of the tonic hit $20 million, mostly because of the Colonel's medicine show.

There were two main reasons for Hadacol's popularity in the teetotaling Bible Belt. First off, Southern Baptists in Louisiana, Arkansas, Alabama and Mississippi all swore by the stuff. They happily testified that it cured every ache and pain known to man and made them feel like a million dollars. The Colonel's customers, who had never tasted alcohol, were bombed and didn't know it.

The second reason for the Hadacol bonanza was Elvis, then a nineteen-year-old guitar player from Memphis whom the Colonel had recruited for the medicine show. The Colonel was quick to notice that when this kid sang, the women in the audience got even more crazy than they had with Hadacol.

Elvis Presley was a rarity among singers in 1954. He

□

was a redneck southerner, like most of those in his audience, but he sang the black man's songs like a black man.
Blues and spirituals were his favorites; a swinging blues like
"That's All Right" was a showstopper, and so was the
plaintive gospel, "A Closer Walk with Thee," a song often
played as a dirge by black bands marching to a funeral and
then swinging on the trip back from the cemetery.

Tom Parker knew that the quickest and surest way to
get national attention for this remarkable new find was to
get him on television. He sent his picture to Gleason, who
recalls his first reaction:

"Marlon Brando was all the rage then. I sensed that
Elvis had the same animal magnetism as Brando. I said that
if this kid could make any kind of noise, let's sign him for
six weeks for our show.

"I sent someone on my staff to see if we could get a
record by this guy. If I remember correctly, we had to send
to Sun Records in Memphis for it. It was 'That's All
Right.'" We had a hell of a time finding it; that's how unknown he was. When I played the record, I saw that his
voice matched his looks. We grabbed him fast.

"Only there was a problem. He was so damn good on
that first show that Tommy and Jimmy [Dorsey] got pissed
off. They argued that they were supposed to be the stars,
not Elvis. Tommy had been through this same thing with
Sinatra. As a result, we only used Elvis a few times, not the
six weeks I wanted."

Hal Wallis, the famed movie producer (*Casablanca*),
saw Elvis on Gleason's show and soon signed him to a
movie contract. RCA bought out his Sun Records contract.
In the spring of 1956, Milton Berle had him on his Tuesday
night show, taped aboard the carrier *Enterprise* at San Diego
Naval Station, where once again Elvis caused a riot with the

□

women. So, by the time Ed Sullivan presented him in the fall of 1956, Elvis was well on his way to superstardom.

Besides introducing Elvis, "Stage Show" cemented the great friendship between Gleason and the Dorseys. No one ever knew the Dorseys better than Gleason, not even the musicians who played for the brothers, whose fights with each other are legendary. Whenever musicians of the Big Band era get together, they talk of terrible-tempered Tommy and his fights with members of his band. Jimmy is always regarded as the milder of the two brothers. Not so, says Jackie:

"I know that of the two brothers, it was always thought Tommy was the Teutonic one, the one with the short fuse. That's only partly true. Jimmy, by far, was the more violent of the two. It was he who always threw the first punch when the two brothers had the knock-down, drag-out fist fights between themselves."

Tommy had a serious drinking problem, as most musicians knew. He often went on binges with Gleason, starting at Toots' bar and winding up at the round house that CBS had built for Gleason in Peekskill. While up there, Jackie and Tommy used to play a bizarre game. They would twirl eggs high up in the air in such a way that they landed unbroken, even on hard surfaces. Tommy held the record; he once twirled an egg over a full-grown tree and it landed with its fragile shell intact.

"It's a game that cannot be played sober," explains Gleason.

In his prime, Tommy would match Gleason drink for drink, sometimes right out of the bottle. Then his doctor made him give it up for a while. Eventually, he went back on white wine, which is commonly used as a rationalization by problem drinkers.

□

"I used to tell Tommy that wine is booze, same as Scotch, but he kept it up and always got just as stoned. That's what finally killed him. He got drunk on white wine and choked to death on his own regurgitation."

When Tommy died in 1956, Jackie took care of all the funeral arrangements. He made a special trip to Shenandoah, Pennsylvania, where he talked to the pastor of the Catholic church the Dorseys had attended for generations. Papa Dorsey was the town's bandmaster and was well respected in the community, and the brothers, along with anthracite coal, had put the town on the map. But no dice. Jackie was told there was no way Tommy could be buried by the Catholic Church, and no way he could be buried in the Dorsey family's consecrated plot in the local Catholic cemetery. Tommy's three wives ruled all that out.

Next stop for Jackie was the chancery office in Scranton, which was Shenandoah's diocese. But he got the same answers when he appealed there.

Jackie then appealed to the charitable instincts of the priest he was dealing with, saying, "How can you call yourself a man of God if you can let a baptized Catholic go to his Maker without even a prayer from his own faith?" At that, the priest personally promised that he would come to the funeral home and recite the rosary outside on the sidewalk during the services.

Tommy was buried by Campbell's Funeral Home in New York, the same place in which Rudolph Valentino had been eulogized some thirty years earlier, while 25,000 fans rioted outside. (The fans had no way of knowing that the family, fearing such adulation, had substituted a wax effigy for the silent screen idol.)

Tommy's funeral caused no such riot, nor even mass adulation. Inside were Gleason, brother Jimmy, Nat (King) Cole and Paul Whiteman, the bandleader who had given

□

the Dorseys their first big-time break. All of them wept when the organist played the great Tommy Dorsey theme, "I'm Getting Sentimental Over You."

And outside was a lone priest from Scranton, quietly saying the rosary.

Jimmy Dorsey lasted only seven months more. He had become paralyzed from a fall, and then developed terminal cancer. Once more, Jackie made the funeral arrangements for a Dorsey brother. As a lapsed Irish Catholic himself, Jackie had felt sad that he hadn't been able to get the Church's official blessing for Tommy. This time he was determined to get a requiem mass for Jimmy, who only had had one wife.

"I didn't go to Shenandoah this time but called St. Patrick's in New York instead. I said I wanted Jimmy buried there and the priest said, 'Upstairs or downstairs?'

"I said, 'What's the difference?' 'No charge downstairs,' said the priest. Somehow this ticked me off. I blew up at the priest, telling him that Jimmy had no visible sins that the Catholic Church could detect and that he had only been married once. Why in the hell couldn't his funeral mass be upstairs for the same price as downstairs? The priest hung up on me."

Gleason next called on his friends in the hierarchy, notably Archbishop Fulton J. Sheen, now an auxiliary bishop of New York. Jimmy was buried upstairs with a full requiem mass. No charge. And no priest outside saying the rosary on the street.

Gleason had been religious as a kid with his Irish mother. He had even been very religious in the first years of his marriage to the devout Gen.

("Hell, we used to say the rosary every night with our arms outstretched.") But the whole Dorsey affair soured him on the Church of his fathers for the next ten years.

□

144

It was not until 1966 that Jack Haley finally talked Jackie into going to mass at the Church of the Good Shepherd in Beverly Hills. The mass had changed from Latin to English, and Jackie admits that he was curious.

"Haley and I are walking in the church and Loretta Young and Irene Dunne, both good Catholics, saw me, turned around and walked out. They thought the roof would cave in.

"Leo Fields, a friend of mine, was driving down Santa Monica Boulevard at the time, and when he saw me going into a church, he crashed his car head-on into a tree."

Despite all of these occurrences, Jackie stayed for the whole mass.

"It was worth it just to hear Haley sing. He thought he was back on Broadway, singing 'Button Up Your Overcoat.' To Haley, a hymn was just another show tune."

As 1956 wound up, so did Jackie's romance with Marilyn. She wanted marriage, and both she and Jackie knew it wasn't meant to happen. They parted friendly, leaving Jackie with no place to go except Toots'. This time, though, he didn't revert to the one-night stands of his youth. Many nights now, he stayed up reading in his penthouse. He was without woman—and a lonely man.

Then, toward the end of 1956, a beautiful girl auditioned for June Taylor as a Gleason showgirl. She did not get involved with Jackie Gleason for some months, but she would become an important part of his life for the next thirteen years.

Let Honey Merrill recall those years: "When I first came on the scene, I heard that Jackie had a romance with Marilyn and that it had cooled. So I became involved with Jackie with my eyes wide open. I knew all about Gen and how she refused to give him a divorce.

□

"But Jackie Gleason is a very easy man to fall in love with. Jackie and I eventually fell in love and we had a very happy thirteen years together, longer than many marriages.

"Much of that time—and people don't know this—Jackie was dry, never touched a drop. He did it all on his own. I never tried to persuade him one way or the other. He would go months at a time without taking one drink. The reason people never knew about it is that Jackie always liked to keep up his image of a heavy drinker.

"I noticed that whenever he did return to drinking during those thirteen years, it always coincided with a return to work. Don't ask me why."

Often, Honey was referred to in print as Jackie's secretary. She did help him with details of his various enterprises, but the "secretary" label was mostly used as a front for the romance. She says, "We talked of marriage often but it was no use. And for all the same reasons. Like the others before me, Jackie and I just drifted apart and I left with no hard feelings.

"I was always very close to Geraldine and Linda, his daughters, and I still keep in touch with them. When my own son [from an earlier marriage] got killed in a motorcycle accident, Jackie called me and was very kind in offering condolences."

When Jackie and Honey began their romance in late 1956, the Gleason CBS-TV show, a Saturday night fixture on the network since 1952, began to decline some in the ratings.

Sadly, the 1956–57 season would see the downfall of two giants of television comedy—Jackie Gleason and Milton Berle. NBC took Berle's Tuesday night domain, an institution since 1948, and gave it to two long-forgotten shows—Jack Webb's "Noah's Ark" and a quiz show called "The Big Surprise." For the first time in nine years, Berle, who had sold more television sets than RCA and Magnavox combined, was without a show.

At the same time, Sid Caesar's "Caesar's Hour" (not to be confused with "Your Show of Shows") also got canceled.

With those three off the air, the Golden Age of Comedy on television had really ended.

▪ 13 ▪
GONE
BUT
NOT
FORGOTTEN

For Jackie Gleason, the years 1957 and 1958 were mostly years of rest and recreation—mostly recreation. And, of course, Jackie could always be found at Toots' bar, where he was still king.

Art Carney left the show when Gleason was canceled and soon was reestablishing himself as a serious actor: on television, in shows like "Playhouse 90" and "Kraft Theater," and in movies and on Broadway. (He would eventually become the original Felix Unger in Neil Simon's *The Odd Couple,* a part not unlike that of the prissy photographer he first played with Gleason in 1950 in the Reggie Van Gleason sketch "Man of Distinction," which had been their first teaming. In movies, Art would go on to such recognition as a Best Actor Oscar in 1975, for *Harry and Tonto.*)

□

On television, meanwhile, the westerns had taken over. Bob Hope, half in jest, said, "Before I can turn on my set, I have to sweep the hay off it." Shows like "Gunsmoke," "Wyatt Earp," "Have Gun, Will Travel" and "Bat Masterson" overwhelmed the usual situation comedies, though a few new ones, such as "Leave it to Beaver" and "The Real McCoys" (starring Walter Brennan and Richard Crenna) survived.

There was another television phenomenon—the big money quiz shows, such as "The $64,000 Question" and "The $64,000 Challenge." Gleason, the serious actor, emerged in a "Studio One" drama *Blood Money,* about what happens to a fellow who wins one of these big TV prizes. Thus, in his year off from "The Jackie Gleason Show," his fans saw another side of the multi-talented Gleason; his serious acting was a revelation to many. But to June Taylor, this was no surprise:

"All of us around Jackie knew of his artistic side. We had seen it in the creation of the symphonic tone poem and ballet "Tawny." Nothing Jackie ever did—or does—surprised any of us close to him."

But Jackie is first of all a comedian, and when the 1958 fall season rolled around, Jackie was back with his variety show. It had the same old beloved characters—except for "The Honeymooners" crew, since Carney was too busy with other acting jobs.

Jackie brought on Buddy Hackett to work with him, mostly during the opening stand-up bits. Buddy is a very funny man in his own right, but there wasn't the chemistry there had been between Gleason and Carney. The filmed episodes of "The Honeymooners" in syndication were getting better ratings than Gleason's own prime-time show.

By New Year's Day, 1959, "The Jackie Gleason Show" was off the air again. The 1958–59 season was a sad

□

one for some of the great comedians. Milton Berle was reduced to emceeing "Jackpot Bowling," while Gracie Allen—who never really liked show business in the first place—retired, leaving George Burns to try it solo. (Burns found himself in the same predicament as Gleason: reruns of the old "Burns and Allen Show" were doing better in the ratings than George's solo effort.)

Even the veteran Ed Wynn, who Jack Benny once said was the funniest man in show business as star of the *Ziegfeld Follies,* was forced to forego comedy for serious drama. Like Gleason, though, Ed excelled in the heavy stuff.

Ed once said, "What the hell kind of a medium is television when Perry Como and Dinah Shore make people laugh and Ed Wynn makes them cry?"

When Jackie left television in 1959, he turned to an old stomping ground—Broadway. David Merrick produced *Take Me Along,* which was the musical-comedy version of Eugene O'Neill's great look at small-town America, *Ah, Wilderness!* Gleason, naturally, was cast as the drinking uncle. What else? He only had thirteen pages of script, but he got such raves from the tough New York critics that it got Jackie his first major acting award—the prestigious Tony.

In this hit musical of 1959, Jackie had once again met up with someone who provided the same sort of chemistry as Art Carney or Audrey Meadows had. This time it was the veteran movie actress Una Merkel, who played the spinster aunt whom Jackie romanced in "Take Me Along," and who is remembered by many as the wise-cracking chorine of such early Warner musicals as *42nd Street,* with Ruby Keeler and Dick Powell.

"She's the greatest actress I have ever worked with," says Jackie." Every line I threw at her, she threw back to me better."

□

The critics, the public and his co-workers—all of them liked Gleason. Everybody, it seemed, liked Gleason but the producer. David Merrick's public disdain of actors is well known, but he took particular delight in going after Jackie.

It all stemmed from a quote of something Gleason said to syndicated columnist Dick Kleiner, who, in 1959, was writing out of New York. (He now writes out of Hollywood.) Kleiner asked Gleason how he liked working for Merrick.

"Merrick works for me," shot back Jackie.

That did it. A few weeks later, Gleason had to miss a few performances because of laryngitis. Merrick told everybody who would listen, "I don't doubt that Jackie has laryngitis, and I also wouldn't be surprised if he stood all night in freezing cold in front of an open window with his pajamas soaked to get it."

What really had ticked off Merrick was Gleason's insistence that early rehearsals be held at Gleason's Round Rock estate at Peekskill. Walter Pidgeon, Ruth Warrick, Una Merkel and the rest of the cast loved rehearsing in the country-club atmosphere. With all its bars, Pidgeon once said he was surprised that the show ever left Peekskill. When the final rehearsals began, Gleason and Honey Merrill made the long trek down the Hudson every day in a chauffeur-driven Rolls-Royce, another CBS perk.

In 1960, after Gleason finished his run in *Take Me Along,* he made a guest appearance on a syndicated Julie Andrews special. In it, he did a solo spot about a working actor who goes out on a cattle-call audition for a part and gets turned down. It was such a brilliant piece of acting that the late Lee Strasberg, the nation's premier drama coach, said that a tape of Gleason's performance should be shown in drama schools everywhere. When reminded of the sketch, Gleason said, "I believe that is the favorite of all the things I have ever done as a serious actor."

Reruns of "The Honeymooners" were shown on stations across the country, and they kept his television comedic image alive. But his hiatus from the medium that had made him a star helped to build a new image of Gleason, as a versatile actor who could walk the tightrope between comedy and tragedy. Jackie comments:

"I have known many comedians—Berle is one—who were superb in serious drama, but there are few serious actors who do comedy well. Cary Grant, William Powell—especially Powell in *My Man Godfrey*—and Jack Lemmon are among the few."

This new, serious Gleason next got the movie role he had been looking for since 1941, playing Minnesota Fats in *The Hustler* opposite Paul Newman and George C. Scott. Gleason's performance is perhaps the one best remembered from that 1961 movie, and it earned him an Academy Award nomination for best supporting actor. (He didn't win, though; this was the year of the *West Side Story* sweep, and dancer George Chakiris got the Oscar.)

(Once again, Gleason was honored outside of television. And yet, he has still never received an Emmy, though both Audrey Meadows and Art Carney have won—Carney, in fact, has won six. Gleason claims that he is not bitter about this, but he never fails to mention it—the last time he did so was on "60 Minutes," in 1985.)

Gleason got some consolation for missing the Oscar in the reviews he received for his performance in *The Hustler*. In September of 1961, Bosley Crowther of *The New York Times* wrote:

"Jackie Gleason is excellent—more so than you at first realize—as a cool, self-collected pool expert who has gone into bondage to the gambling man (Scott). His deceptively casual behavior in that titanic initial game conceals a pathetic robot that you only later perceive."

Gleason had some interesting experiences in the making of *The Hustler.* Not knowing that Scott was fighting to lick a drinking problem, Jackie was always inviting him out to some bar or another. This was shortly after a well-publicized incident at the Beverly Hills Polo Lounge, when George was drinking with Ava Gardner, also a lover of fine wines. Toward the end of the evening, George ordered a bottle of Dom Perignon 1959, the finest vintage in years. Then, according to the police report, he took the bottle and was about to open it on Ava's head. Fortunately, a couple of waiters and a security officer prevented Ava from being used as a corkscrew.

"I have always admired the class of a guy who would order the best wine in the house to hit a woman over the head with," says Jackie. "Most guys in my old neighborhood would have used a cheap bottle of muscatel in a brown paper sack to do the job."

Paul Newman was coached by Gleason's pal, champion Willie Mosconi, and he got so he could shoot a pretty good game of pool. As Jackie tells it:

"He got a little cocky and challenged the old Brooklyn pool hustler to a game of pocket billiards, fifty count. I asked him, 'for how much?' Paul said fifty bucks sounded about right. He got to break the balls. I then ran fifty balls straight. He never got a chance to chalk his cue.

"The bastard got even with me, though. Next day, he paid me off with a jar filled with five thousand pennies."

Gleason, once a television presence, was fast becoming known as a movie star. Besides *The Hustler,* he also made the Chaplinesque *Gigot* in Paris. In *Gigot,* in which he played the saddest of clowns, Jackie wrote both the story and the musical score, but he let Gene Kelly do the direct-

□

ing. It's Gleason's favorite among his movie roles, although to many it had a little too much pathos.

"I don't buy this stuff that great comedy comes out of great tragedy, or that you have to be lonely to have talent," Jackie says. But a look at *Gigot* somehow contradicts that. Compared with movies in which Gleason did comedy, *Gigot* was not all that successful. Audiences didn't like Ralph Kramden or Reggie Van Gleason making them cry or feel sad. And the cost of *Gigot,* a whopping $5 million, was excessive for 1961. Gene Kelly recalls the making of *Gigot*:

"When we were making it, Jackie and I thought we had a classic going for us. Jackie owned the property but he didn't own the rights to the final cut. When Ken Hyman and Ray Stark—or somebody at Seven Arts—got through cutting it, it was not the picture I directed. It was good but not great, as it could have been. I did have a wonderful time working with Jackie, though, and we are still great friends. He always had Milton Berle, Orson Welles, and me open his seasons when his television show was in Miami Beach."

Jackie's expensive tastes had a lot to do with the big budget. As soon as he arrived in Paris for the shooting, he hired a hundred-piece symphony orchestra to record the score he had written. The production manager frantically called the money men in New York; there was no budget provision for such an expense. But Gleason got his big symphony orchestra.

One small scene was shot in a church. Gleason wanted a certain kind of a church, but Paris, with all of its Notre Dames and Sacre Coeurs, didn't have the kind Jackie liked. So he built his own church for the scene, and churches don't come cheap.

Working in Paris and eating all that French food led

Jackie to a remarkable restaurant. "After a while all those rich sauces get tiresome. I knew Gene Kelly had spent a lot of time in Paris, so I asked him one day if there was one restaurant in that town where you could get plain, substantial food, preferably American.

"Right away, Kelly took me over to LeRoy Haines' restaurant in Montmartre. LeRoy was a black chef from Chicago who went to Paris and opened a restaurant that featured barbecued pork ribs, Texas chili and homemade apple pie. After my first visit there, I had an embossed certificate made that stated: 'Winner of the First Annual Jackie Gleason Culinary Award.' It still hangs in LeRoy's restaurant."

But Jackie hung out at the fancy places, too. Claude Terrail, who owned the famous Tour D'Argent, always seated Jackie next to a corner window and gave him a few extra tables to ensure dining in privacy.

"I was sitting there alone one night and who should come in but Jack L. Warner, with about twelve people. He spotted me and said, 'Hey, I once had you under contract' and invited me to join him.

"He had just broken the bank at Monte Carlo and spent about sixteen or seventeen thousand dollars for dinner."

Gleason says, "Jack *was* a frustrated comic. I heard him use one liners that I hadn't heard since the days when I emceed amateur shows at the Halsey."

Jackie had another confrontation with a studio boss in Paris—Darryl Zanuck. Gleason had Zanuck's suite at the George V, and when Zanuck came to town, he called Gleason and told him, "I've got to have my suite. My girlfriend [Juliette Greco, the actress darling of the Sartre Existentialists of the Left Bank] loves that suite. If you give it to me, I'll see that you have the finest suite at the Plaza

Athenée, all on me." But Jackie didn't give up his suite at the George V—and he never worked for Zanuck.

After *Gigot* was finished, Gleason came back to Hollywood and did *Soldier in the Rain* with Steve McQueen. McQueen was a tough guy to work with, but Gleason had his respect.

One day singer Bobby Darin was moaning to Jackie how difficult McQueen was. "I think," said Jackie, "that Steve is his own worst enemy."

Darin, who had just done a movie with McQueen, answered, "Not while I'm alive."

In 1962, Jackie did two memorable movies. The first was *Requiem for a Heavyweight,* in which he portrayed the fight manager, with Tony Quinn. Mickey Rooney was also in that movie, and Jackie is lavish in his praise of Rooney the actor. "If Rooney had been born six feet tall, he would be Lord Laurence Olivier," says Jackie.

And then he got another part in a movie that was right up his alley. It was *Papa's Delicate Condition,* the story of silent screen star Corinne Griffith's eccentric drinking father, which was directed by the late George Marshall, rated one of Hollywood's greatest directors of comedy (*Destry Rides Again, You Can't Cheat an Honest Man,* et cetera).

George once said this about Jackie Gleason in one scene of *Papa's Delicate Condition*:

"In my fifty years in the business [Marshall and John Ford both started directing the same day in 1914], I have only twice seen an actor steal a scene from a child. Jackie did it with his back to the camera and still stole the whole scene. Once before W. C. Fields did it with Baby LeRoy— Bill put gin in Baby LeRoy's orange juice—but Bill stole his scene by facing the camera. Jackie did it the hard way. He put the gin in his own orange juice."

It was during the making of *Papa's Delicate Condition*

□

157

that Jackie accosted me on the Paramount lot and invited me into his dressing room for a drink. "Pallie," he said, "how would you like to take a train trip across country with me? It's the only way to fly."

And for Jackie, it was. When the movie finished, Jackie chartered a train to make a ten-day trip across country to Toots Shor's bar in New York. CBS-TV footed the bill, because Jackie was about to make his return to Saturday night television, in the fall of 1962. The network allowed Jackie to invite his drinking buddies along on the trip, plus those beautiful showgirls who always opened the Gleason show. In return for CBS-TV picking up the tab, Jackie agreed to make stops at key cities along the way to plug his return to Saturday night television. At that time, though, CBS-TV had no idea that such a trip would cost $100,000.

The send-off party at Union Station in downtown Los Angeles was hard to top. Besides the beautiful showgirls, two Dixieland bands, including Max Kaminsky's band— which Gleason had flown out from New York—were blasting away, both inside the train and outside on the platform. ("Max always plays for me on trains," explained Gleason.) Also out on the station platform were clowns, midget Billy Curtis (dressed as a miniature Reggie Van Gleason) and Colonel Tom Parker, without Elvis.

Some movie-star friends of Jackie's showed up to give him a send-off, and George Marshall almost went along on the trip. Jackie did his best to kidnap the director and at one point had him locked in a bathroom. It was that kind of party.

Jackie himself was resplendent in a grey suit with a red vest and a red carnation in his lapel. He was gorgeous, and one could see why Cary Grant had once called him the most stylish man in show business.

□

Billy the midget, as tiny Reggie, greeted each guest as they boarded the train for the party. Colonel Parker, true to form, was selling autographed pictures of Gleason on the platform.

"Twenty-five cents. Pay no more," hawked the onetime carnival barker. He sold out quickly with the Gleason pictures. Then the Colonel, not so mysteriously, started selling autographed pictures of his boy Elvis.

"Fifty cents. Pay no more!" he shouted. These sold even faster than Gleason's, because the platform soon was filled with a crowd of bobby-soxers ogling the stars. When the Colonel had sold all his Presley photos, he miraculously produced a gas cylinder and hundreds of balloons with Elvis' face imprinted on them. Billy the midget was helping him blow up the balloons.

Then a bizarre thing happened. Billy was holding too many balloons, and suddenly, the little guy was rising off the ground.

Gleason spotted little Reggie heading skyward, and rushed out and grabbed him by the legs. "It's a good thing I caught him," said Jackie. "He would have beaten this train into San Bernardino by half an hour."

Then Gleason took his first drink in three days—a triple screwdriver. "I went into training for this trip, just like Muhammad Ali [who was better known as Cassius Clay in those days]," said Jackie.

Some forty-five people went along for the train ride, a normal Gleason entourage. The route was set to follow a zigzag course across the country in order to hit the key television markets—Phoenix, Denver, St. Louis, Chicago, Pittsburgh, Baltimore, Philadelphia and New York—where they all headed for Toots' bar for a wind-up party.

CBS may have thought of these stops as promotion, but Jackie called them "fresh-ice stops." He had a theory

□

that most hangovers are caused by stale ice. Jackie was off his usual Scotch for the trip, but was very big with orange juice and vodka.

Just before the train pulled out of Union Station three hours late, old pal Jack Haley came aboard. Jack made another frantic appeal for Gleason to forego his evil ways and return to the faith of his Irish forebears.

"I know a priest who will forgive anything in confession—and no lectures, sermons or questions," said the devout Haley. Max Kaminsky commented: "I'd pay ten thousand bucks to hear that first confession."

Gleason listened politely to Haley's pitch and said, "One of these days, pal."

Haley, sensing that this was neither the time nor the place for the return of a prodigal son, then asked Jackie to buy two tickets, at a hundred bucks per plate, for a dinner to help raise funds for Father Patrick Peyton and his Family Rosary Crusade ("The Family that Prays Together Stays Together"). Haley was chairman of the dinner honoring the Irish-born priest.

Gleason took out his checkbook and wrote a check for $10,000 and, with a Reggie Van Gleason flourish, handed it to the astonished Haley.

"Use it to buy tickets for priests and nuns who can't afford to pay a C-note for dinner," said Gleason.

On that religious note, the conductor yelled, "All aboard!" and the train chugged out of Union Station. To the crowd waiting outside on the platform, Jackie gave his famous "Awa-a-a-a-y We Go!" yell and "Traveling Music" kick.

Max Kaminsky's Six Original Arabian Kettle Drum Kickers blasted out with "Chattanooga Choo-Choo." Also staying on board were June Taylor and some of her dancers; the beautiful showgirls, called Glea Girls, who opened

□

every Gleason show; some CBS executives; Sue Ane Langdon, the new Alice Kramden (Audrey Meadows had retired to get married); Jackie's longtime secretary Sydell Spear, and I. All the ingredients were there for a first-class orgy. We had wine, women and song, not necessarily in that order. The train was filled with bedrooms, but it was a circumspect trip all the way. Except for the drinking aboard, Gleason was always a stern father with the girls. When the drinking would get a little rough, Jackie would give a sign to June Taylor and she would herd the girls back to their compartments.

Their sleeping quarters were off limits, and the girls had all been warned against any hanky-panky, which would have meant instant dismissal and an airline ticket home at the next stop. With the girls gone to bed, the club car turned into an Irish pub-on-wheels, complete with New Orleans jazz. It was happy hour for the hard-core serious drinkers.

Somewhere in the middle of the Mojave Desert, Jackie waved to Max and told him to take five. Believe it or not, the band had been playing continually for eight hours straight. The Irish hour had begun.

Jack Philbin, the producer, started playing the piano in the club car, and Walter Stone, the writer and resident Irish tenor, sang "Galway Bay," two or three times in a row. It was Jackie's favorite, reminding him of his childhood, when his mother used to hold him in her arms and sing him Irish lullabies. Walter had just enough whiskey in him to sound good, and fortunately, so did his audience. As Walter sang, Gleason rested his elbows on the piano top and listened with the same facial expressions Joe the Bartender used when he listened to Crazy Guggenheim sing. Jackie was in that sentimental mood, common to most Irishmen who are drinking, and you could tell that "Galway Bay" was a precious song. Jackie never moved except to raise the glass to his lips. Walter knew his boss's moods—and also all the traditional Irish songs.

Then, as suddenly as it started, the Irish Hour was over. Jackie became Reggie again and danced down the aisle. Max took this as the cue to blast out with "Strutters Ball."

"Mmmmm, you're a good group," said Jackie, and once again, it was New Year's Eve. Outside, it was a beautiful night, with a harvest moon illuminating the vast desert. The train must have been doing ninety miles per hour, almost as fast as the bartender was serving drinks. By this time, it was well past midnight, and with all the excitement going on, no one had thought about food. Now, Gleason, with that gargantuan appetite, thought about it. A dining car steward was summoned.

"Let's have about a dozen barbecued baby pork ribs, pal," said Gleason, disdaining the printed menu. He could have gotten pheasant under Rolls-Royce hubcaps more easily—there were no ribs in the galley. When told this, Gleason immediately assumed a Poor Soul look of disappointment. It threw some of his staff into near panic, but not Sydell, the secretary. She was used to crises with Gleason. Jackie called her over and said, "Sydell, where can we get some ribs?"

The train was somewhere between Barstow and Needles in the California desert, and you just can't pull a train into an all-night diner. The only ribs out there were probably still on coyotes howling in the night.

"It might take a little time, Jackie," said Sydell. "Maybe an hour or so."

Sydell is one of those resourceful secretaries that employers dream about. Jackie hired her on the spot in 1958, after interviewing dozens of applicants, by the way she answered one stock question. Jackie asked her if she knew shorthand.

"Yes, but it takes me longer," said Sydell.

Bizarre requests from Jackie were nothing new to her. Once he had asked her to get the Pope on the phone during a drinking session. In minutes, she had an Italian cardinal in the Vatican and handed the phone to Jackie. He never got the Pope, though, because the cardinal spoke no English and Jackie spoke no Italian.

Later, in 1964, he wanted the President. Sydell thought he meant Jim Aubrey, then president of CBS-TV. When Aubrey got on the phone, Jackie said he'd meant the President of the United States—Lyndon B. Johnson. In seconds, Sydell had an undersecretary of state apologizing because LBJ was in a cabinet meeting. He promised that LBJ, a Gleason fan, would call back—and he did.

So, getting ribs in the middle of the Mojave Desert was no big deal for Sydell. She soon was conferring with the conductor, and within minutes the train pulled into one of those godforsaken tank-stop sidings. Sydell, the conductor and the steward got off the train and went into the little section shed beside the railroad tracks. Soon the staccato of a Morse telegraph key punctuated the desert silence. The trio got back on the train, a whistle was blown, and the Gleason Sour Mash Express was chugging along on the main line of the Southern Pacific.

Max celebrated the occasion with a somewhat stirring rendition of "Tiger Rag." You could see why Gleason always had this band on his train.

About an hour later, the train pulled into the station at Needles, on the California-Arizona border. There, standing on the platform, was a little Chinese waiter with a half dozen greasy boxes, three to an arm, waiting. Gleason had his ribs, and they were exceptionally good.

□

"Now was that so damn hard?" asked Jackie of his astonished guests.

Around 5 A.M., the party in the club car started petering out. It had begun at 4 P.M. the previous day, and Max's band was starting to play waltzes. Somehow, we all made it to our sleeping quarters for a few hours of sleep before Phoenix, our first stop for a civic reception and fresh ice for our drinks.

At 8 A.M., an hour before arrival, I was in the dining car. Gleason followed shortly, nursing a monumental hangover that was very visible to the naked red eye.

Jackie glanced at the breakfast menu. Special of the day was fried calf's brains. It's typical ranch fare for the Southwest, but it's a terrible thing to face in the morning when you look like a bad embalming job, as Jackie did.

Jackie cocked his head sideways and then, with that sweeping arm gesture, right index finger pointed upward, he shouted, "First guy who orders this, off the train!" Jackie then ordered two screwdrivers back to back and some bacon and eggs. The screwdrivers, he explained, were rich in Vitamin C.

The train stopped and Jackie, holding his big head in his hands, barely made it to the train door. There were thousands of people out there all yelling and screaming, "How sweet it is!" and "Awa-a-a-a-y we go!"

The politicians who had staged the welcome meant well, but, considering Jackie's condition, they never should have invited those crazy cowboys and Indians from Williams, Arizona. These guys didn't only stage a welcome; they staged the Gun Fight at the O.K. Corral on horseback. Such noise!

Gleason was dying inside, but he was a good sport about the welcome, charming and affable, as well as touched.

□

The date was August 10, 1962, and at 9 A.M. in Phoenix, the sun was hot and the temperature must have been around 110 degrees. Great hangover weather. Whenever Gleason told a joke from the train platform, the cowboys and Indians would shoot off their guns and let out the most gawd-awful war whoops. It was the wildest reception Gleason ever got anyplace. Worse, Jackie had to listen to all the politicians talk. Then there were the scrolls to be read, with their endless whereases. The sun was boiling Gleason's bare head.

Finally, relief came in a fleet of air-conditioned Cadillac limousines. As Gleason hurried to one, an official stopped him. "We have a special conveyance for you, Jackie."

Out of an alley came a six-horse team pulling a real stage coach. Gleason, still with the hangover, bounced the eight miles to the hotel, riding shotgun on the stage.

It was a John Wayne welcome. The cowboys and Indians rode alongside on their horses, shooting off their guns at the slightest excuse. It was obvious that the cowboys and Indians had had some early morning firewater. Gleason had barely put on his bathrobe after a shower at the hotel when the wild men stormed into his room. Happily, they had run out of ammunition, so the guns were silenced.

The wild westerners finally left, but there was no time for Gleason to take a much-needed nap. At the official civic luncheon in a downtown auditorium, Jackie ordered about three screwdrivers, insisting that only freshly squeezed orange juice be used. To Jackie's credit, he never refused a drink.

"People expect it of me," he would say, ordering another double vodka and orange juice. At the luncheon, Jackie was in rare form as he said, "The governor just told me his salary is eighteen thousand dollars a year. That wouldn't buy the olives in my martinis." Then he gave his views on drinking: "I'm no alcoholic. I'm a drunkard. There's a difference. A drunkard doesn't like to go to meetings."

Then a hometown combo entertained, featuring a gangly seventeen-year-old kid with a high-pitched voice, who sang "Danny Boy" as only a high tenor can. He was a big hit, especially with Gleason. Gleason announced from the head table: "You guys are on my first five shows."

I was sitting with Jack Philbin, the producer. "We're booked solid for the first ten," said Philbin.

But the hometown combo did five shows with Jackie, and the Gleason show started the seventeen-year-old high-voiced singer on his way to becoming the Las Vegas millionaire he is today. His name was Wayne Newton.

Before the day was over, Gleason had met and chatted with half of Phoenix. Finally, around 10 P.M., we were all back in the club car. The train was due to depart for Denver around midnight. Max's band, which had been playing most of thirty hours, was still giving out with the hot Dixieland jazz. It looked like another of those nights, but then a funny thing happened. The band literally collapsed. It had blown itself out. This didn't stop Gleason. He had Sydell bring out some albums, mostly his own. It was music to drink by.

Someplace in that stack of records was David Rose's great original burlesque song "The Stripper." This music was so dirty, so low-down in its beat, that Jackie was immediately taken back to the Empire Burlesque Theatre in Newark. In a bit of Chaplinesque pantomime, he loosened his necktie and grabbed both ends of it. Working the unknotted tie, he somehow created an illusion of a stripper on a runway doing bumps and grinds. It was comedy at its finest.

□

When the burlesque music stopped, so did Jackie. He knew he couldn't top that performance. He rose and walked slowly down the aisle toward his compartment. As he reached the door, he shot a backward glance at the rest of us and said, "You're nice people." It was The Poor Soul speaking and making his exit.

I sat there for a few minutes and soon the Golden State Limited stopped alongside us. It was headed for Los Angeles where, sadly, I was due back at work the following morning. I hurriedly grabbed my bag and got on the train.

The next morning I sent a wire to meet Jackie in Denver, explaining: "Sorry, but I had to leave with the first wounded." This wire, I later found, so unnerved Jackie that he didn't take a drink the rest of the trip—until the final party at Toots'.

· 14 ·
THE
END
OF
AN
ERA

The biggest television hit of 1962 was the return of Jackie Gleason to Saturday night television, with very little change from his old format. True, there was a new Alice in Sue Ane Langdon and a new Trixie in Patricia Wilson, neither of whom would last the season. But the show was vintage Gleason.

No doubt the publicity the train trip had created contributed to the ratings, which were higher than usual. Jackie had all his old fans, plus college kids who were mere children when Jackie had started a dozen years earlier on Dumont's "Cavalcade of Stars."

Forgotten was the previous year's fiasco, "You're in the Picture," a game show thought up by some CBS executives who wanted to make sure that Gleason earned that

□

$100,000 per year they were paying for his exclusive services, whether he worked or not.

"This show was such a disaster that I draw a blank every time I try to explain the format. It had something to do with identifying celebrities' pictures," says Jackie. "The only good show was the second one, in which I apologized for the first one."

Gleason's apology was in the nature of a stand-up comedy routine and it was hilarious. A half hour of apologizing is hard comedy to do but Gleason pulled it off.

In the 1962 return to CBS, all the Gleason characters went to work again, but within a new framework called "The American Scene Magazine." The new format was a series of blackouts, short, fast sketches, ending almost as fast as they began. (Some years later, "Rowan and Martin's Laugh-In" would use a similar format with great success.)

Sue Ane Langdon had left a husband back in California and didn't take too well to the New York taping. She left the show before the season ended, and Jackie sidelined "The Honeymooners," concentrating on the other sketches. Gleason himself wasn't all that crazy about taping in New York, since he had become a golf addict, and you can't play golf in the wintertime in New York. In 1963, he casually mentioned to columnist Earl Wilson that he would like to play golf year round, perhaps in some warm place like southern California.

That item quickly caught the eye of Hank Meyer, the public-relations man for Miami Beach. Hank got his client to offer Gleason the moon over Miami if he would move his show down there. One of the inducements was a new home, right on a fairway of the Miami Beach Country Club. In 1964, Gleason moved out of New York forever. Of course, it meant another one of those crazy train trips, this one from New York to Miami. He went directly from

□

the train to his home on the golf course. His office was attached to the house and looked out onto a fairway. Another perk was a private golf cart built like a miniature Rolls-Royce. It had radio, television and turn signals. It also was kept well stocked with chilled Dom Perignon, Scotch, vodka, gin, olives, mixers and all the other accoutrements of a rolling Toots Shor's. The comedian, who just fifteen years before had starred in "The Life of Riley," was now really living it.

Southern Florida, from Palm Beach down to Key West, got more out of Jackie than they gave him in fringe benefits. For the next five years, the show would proclaim itself as originating "from the sun and fun capital of the world." You couldn't beat the show's opening shot, which showed the blue Atlantic under billowing white clouds and azure skies, highlighting both the Miami and Miami Beach shorelines. It was the biggest thing to happen in Florida since the land boom of the twenties.

Hank Meyer, who engineered the move, must have thought he had gone to press agents' heaven. Jackie's viewers, imprisoned in heated homes with blizzards raging outside, were dreaming of spending the winter in Florida.

One of Jackie's first guests in 1964 was his idol Buster Keaton, who came down just two years before his death. Jackie observes: "Chaplin had one character—the little tramp—and he stuck with it to great critical acclaim and financial success, but for sheer comedic creativity, he wasn't in the same league with Buster Keaton.

"Buster came on my show and got a little drunk. My producers wanted to cancel him. I would sooner have canceled myself. I got him sober and he did the show and was a tremendous hit."

Milton Berle became almost a regular guest in the Florida days. "I must have done twenty appearances for him in Florida," Milton recalls. "And he always paid me twenty thousand a shot. I don't know of anyone else who got that kind of money."

Milton is the ultimate perfectionist, and he was the only star in history who ever got Gleason to rehearse with him. Milton remembers:

"I told him, 'You bastard, you are going to rehearse with me all week. None of this no-show-until-airtime stuff with me.'"

(Milton could also insult Gleason and get away with it. With Gleason weighing in at 280 pounds, Berle introduced Jackie as "my three favorite comedians.")

All of this rehearsing amazed Gleason's staff, many of whom had been with him since the Dumont days. With Berle, there was none of that "every man for himself" routine.

But Berle was the only one who got special treatment. The veteran comedian and game show host Jan Murray recalls his experience on a 1965 show:

"The show was taped live on Friday nights, but Jackie's people wanted me in Florida the Monday before. First question I asked was, 'Where's Jackie?' 'On the golf course,' someone answered. 'What's this? The nineteenth hole at the Miami Beach Country Club is Toots Shor's with sunshine?'

"As it got closer to airtime, I wonder, what is this? Am I working with Claude Rains, the invisible man? All week, there are run-throughs and rehearsals, with Jack Philbin the producer standing in for Jackie. Finally, on Thursday night, twenty-four hours before taping, I ran into Jackie in a Miami Beach bar. Where else? I yelled at him, 'Hey, phantom!' Jackie patted me on the back and said, 'Don't worry, pal. You will be great.'"

Jan was worried, because when the show aired on Sat-

Scene from William Saroyan's *The Time of Your Life*, which Jackie did for CBS-TV in the fifties. Standing is a young Jack Klugman, and seated is Dick York.

Jackie's fiftieth birthday party, in 1966. Back row, left to right: famed jockey Eddie Arcaro, Art Carney, Alan King, grid great Paul Hornung, Whitey Ford, Frankie Avalon, Frank Gorshin. Bottom row, left to right: Gene Kelly, Jack Haley, Sheila MacRae, Lucille Ball, Jackie, Archbishop Fulton J. Sheen, Danny Thomas, and Sammy Spear.

This is actually the name of a prominent street in Miami Beach.

Jackie, a better-than-average golfer, tees off in a Florida golf match with stone-faced Ed Sullivan, who is worrying about a bet he has just made with The Great One.

Jackie shows off his new home base, the Miami Beach Civic Auditorium, in 1964—when the Gleason show moved out of New York forever.

Above: Jackie is the one on the left. No wonder Gleason called his office in the Park Sheraton penthouse "The Elephant Room."

Right: This was Jackie's dressing room on the Paramount set of *Papa's Delicate Condition,* and that's director George Marshall in the doorway. Notice the bar on this usually dry lot back in 1962 when the bossman at Paramount was Y. Frank Freeman, a noted abstainer. (No wonder—he was one of the biggest stockholders in Coca-Cola.)

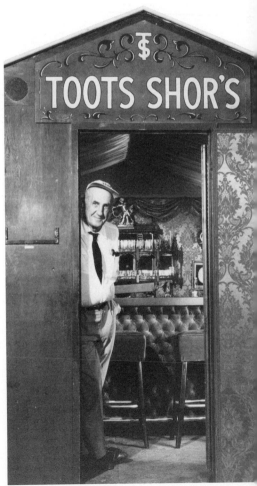

Two American institutions. Bob Hope and Jackie when Gleason appeared on Hope's NBC-TV show during the sixties.

Above: A collector's item. Toots Shor at the Automat, pouring himself a cup of coffee. No alcohol in sight.

Right: Reggie Van Gleason the Third wasn't always a playboy. He loved sports, too.

Above: "Is this the Pope?" Jackie, when drinking, sometimes gets telephonitis.

Right: This was Jackie's fighting weight around 1971, when he left weekly television for good. He really meant it when he said, "And away we go!"

Right: Jackie and fellow actor do a movers sketch on the Gleason show back in the early CBS-TV days of the fifties.

Below: Reggie Van Gleason the Third, with Art Carney as his father and Zahma Cunningham as his mother.

Right: Jackie and June Taylor at work with her dancers. Jackie had a hand in everything on his television show.

"And here's the star of our show, Jackie Gleason." One of television's most famous entrances, staged with the help of the June Taylor dancers.

This is what you call high-priced harmony. Alan King, Liberace, Jackie, and Bing Crosby do a little barbershop singing on the Gleason show during the sixties.

Gene Kelly and Jackie, two legendary Irishmen, ham it up with Brigitte Bardot.

Jackie and Art doing a Laurel and Hardy routine on "The Honeymooners." Joyce Randolph is playing the "ever-popular Mae Busch" in the skit.

Left: Pert Kelton, the original Alice Kramden when "The Honeymooners" made its debut in 1950 on the old Dumont network. Pert returned in the sixties to play Alice's mother on the show.

Below: Loud Mouth Charlie Bratton, an early Gleason character of the fifties, gives it to the Caspar Milquetoasty Art Carney.

Left: Audrey Meadows, the most famous of the four Alice Kramdens.

Below: Ed Norton, about to enter his office in the New York Department of Sewers.

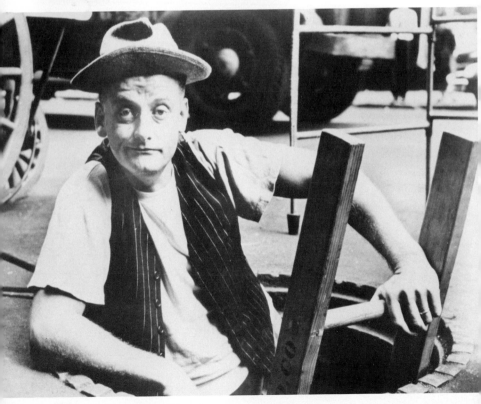

Above: Ed Norton and Ralph Kramden in the Austrian Alps, when "The Honeymooners" went abroad in the sixties.

Right: Ed and Ralph in Italy. Gleason looks like a fat Chico Marx in this getup.

Left: Olé! Jackie ("Manolete") Gleason about to face the bull in a "Honeymooners" sketch of the sixties set in Spain.

Below: Bwana Gleason about to shoot leopards on an African safari—if he doesn't get shot first in that outfit, a reject from Abercrombie and Fitch.

Facing page, top: "The Honeymooners" land in jail. Sheila MacRae, Jane Kean, Art Carney, and the unperturbed Gleason.

Facing page, bottom: "I tell you, Norton. My no-cal pizza will make us both rich." Jackie as Ralph Kramden and Art Carney as Ed Norton from a "Honeymooners" reunion.

Mmmm! That's good coffee. Jackie often
drank coffee on the air that was 100 proof.

urday night, he was afraid he would die in front of fifty million people. "I have died before with my act, but I always died well rehearsed.

"I don't see Jackie until a few hours before we tape that Friday night for airing Saturday. He comes over to me and says, 'Okay, pal. What are you and I supposed to do?'

"What am I supposed to do? It's his show. He should be telling me what we're doing. Now the flop sweat is forming on my forehead as I start reading him some stuff I had prepared on how to swing a golf club. He said, 'I like that.' And then he asked about physical action. I told him. I have spoken more words in saying 'Hello' to a stranger. 'Gotcha, pal,' he said. That was our rehearsal. I knew I was going to die out on that stage, but what the hell, I at least got a good tan out of my week without Gleason.

"A minute before airtime, Gleason uttered the words I had been dreading. 'Every man for himself.' I think that's what the captain of the *Titanic* said before it sunk. Taping begins and Jackie walks out in front of that Miami Beach audience. He is the king. The audience is screaming.

"Our sketch comes on. Remember, I only had read the lines to Jackie. That was the extent of his knowledge of the script. Well, he knows the lines better than I do—and I wrote them! How he does it, I honestly don't know. When I got back to Beverly Hills, my wife Toni says, 'Jan, you and Gleason should be a team. You were like Laurel and Hardy together.'"

Gleason explained why he rehearsed with Milton, and not with Jan. "I had to do it with Milton because he brought along material enough to do a Broadway show. But I guess it's because his name was up in lights there in Times Square when I was eating my waffle with apple butter and only had twenty-one cents left to my name."

By the 1966–67 season, Jackie was earning $205,000

□

per week, plus another $720,000 for a summer replacement show. The fall of 1966 also marked the revival of "The Honeymooners"; CBS had been pressured by thousands of fan letters to bring back the Kramdens and Nortons. Art Carney was available, but Audrey Meadows and Joyce Randolph were not, except for a 1966 special called "The Adoption," the last black-and-white episode ever filmed. The search was on.

Finding Trixie was easy. Gleason got Jane Kean, an old friend of Gleason's whose sister Betty was married to Gleason's old chum Lew Parker. At one time, Jackie and the Kean sisters had even talked about doing an act together.

"It never worked out," Jane recalls, "because Jackie didn't have a stand-up act at the time."

Jackie found his Alice in Sheila MacRae, then wife of singer Gordon MacRae. Sheila had been an actress, but she had given it all up to rear the MacRae children—one of whom is actress Meredith MacRae. When the children got bigger, Sheila joined Gordon's act and became a tremendous asset. Gleason caught the act one night in a Miami Beach hotel and knew right away that he had his new Alice.

Sheila recalls how she was hired to become the fourth and final Alice.

"I had always adored Jackie. In fact, I idolized him even while I was waiting for Gordon for hours in Toots Shor's when Jackie was drinking with my husband. At that time, I had two good ones on my hands. [Gordon since has become a recovered alcoholic.]

"Jackie caught our act in Florida many times, but what really cinched the job for me was when I played Miss Adelaide to Alan King's Nathan Detroit in the revival of *Guys and Dolls*.

□

"Next thing I knew—Gordon and I had separated by this time—I got a call about two or three in the morning from Jackie in Florida.

"'Clam,' he said, 'I'm thinking about doing about fifteen 'Honeymooners' with different Alices. He named off a whole list of actresses, including Audrey. And he wanted me to do one or two.

"I called my agent, who said I still had a firm equity contract and it was impossible. Besides, he said I was too much of a jet-setter. That's what *Variety* had called me in their review of *Guys and Dolls*.

"That made me all the more determined to go down to Florida and talk with Jackie. So I called him and said, 'Send me the ticket.'"

Sheila was to find herself part of the continuing saga of Gleason's unusual hiring practices.

"I was a little apprehensive flying down because I didn't have red hair like Audrey and then it hit me. All of Audrey's shows were in black and white, so the red hair didn't show. Then when I met with Jackie, he asked me if I believed in ESP. I told him I did.

"Okay, pick a number between one and twenty-five. I said seven. He said, 'Right. You will hear from me.' I didn't know—and I'll never know—whether I picked the right number or not, but I got on Northeast Airlines and flew back to New York. As soon as I stepped off the plane, all I could hear over the JFK intercom was 'Sheila MacRae, please pick up the Northeast courtesy phone.' There was a message to call Jackie immediately. I did. He said he wanted me for all fifteen shows."

(It's interesting to note that Sheila thinks Gleason is the perfect Hamlet. One night in Toots Shor's, Gleason and the noted critic Brooks Atkinson got in an argument about acting. Atkinson said no actor was worth his salt un-

□

less he could do the Prince of Denmark. Gleason, well fortified with Scotch, did the soliloquy from *Hamlet* letter perfect before the astonished critic and an even more astonished Toots and the rest of the diners. The late Paul Douglas, himself a noted actor, once said: "John Barrymore couldn't have done it better." Jackie says it is the one and only time he ever did Shakespeare in public.)

The plan for "The Honeymooners" was to take the characters out of the Brooklyn tenement, even so far as to Europe, and to make the show into a musical. In Sheila and Jane, you had two women who could sing. Perfect.

For nostalgia's sake, Jackie brought back the original Alice, Pert Kelton, to play Mrs. Gibson, Alice's mother. "I didn't lose a daughter. I gained a ton," said Pert, with all the old fire she had as Alice back in the Dumont days.

Jackie's romance with Honey Merrill ended in 1969. The parting was friendly, but it ended for the same reason that Jackie's romance with Marilyn Taylor had ended—no hope of marriage.

Honey moved to Las Vegas, where she married Dick Roman, a well-known Las Vegas singer.

Jackie had Virginia Grey on the show in Miami Beach for a vignette. She long had been known as Clark Gable's favorite girlfriend, but he never married her. Virginia was an accomplished actress, and Jackie fell for her in more ways than one.

"Our romance was very innocent. We used to do fun things like roller skating. First time I ever got on a rink with her, I fell flat on my derriere. If it hadn't been for two sailors who lifted me up, I would still be lying there. I was a little hefty in those days."

Virginia told him: "If you had been an expert skater

☐

like you are an expert everything else, I never could have loved you."

That romance was short-lived; Virginia, like Gen and Marilyn, was a devout Catholic and saw no hope of marriage. (She had fallen for Gable when she was a young contract player at MGM and Gable was the biggest star in the business. She didn't want to repeat the girlfriend act now.)

Virginia went back to California. The Gleason show, now with the musical "Honeymooners," was getting big ratings. So were the filmed reruns. One station—WPIX, New York—ran them every night, over and over.

Naturally, the success of "The Honeymooners" spawned imitators. Hanna-Barbera produced "The Flintstones," a cartoon version of the Kramdens in the Stone Age. In England, showing simultaneously with the musical "Honeymooners" on the Gleason show was "Coronation Street"—the Kramdens transplanted to Manchester, with the same working-stiff background.

Most famous of all the imitators, however, was the very successful "All in the Family," starring Carroll O'Connor as Archie Bunker. Carroll once wrote Jackie: "I know I am doing some of the things you did."

Jackie wrote back: "I wish I had done some of the things you're doing."

In Florida during the late sixties, Jackie introduced another star—the late Frank Fontaine, father of twelve kids and a longtime showstopper, even when he had been on radio with Jack Benny. Frank had developed a punch-drunk act that was a natural for the part of Crazy Guggenheim (a character based on a member of Gleason's boyhood gang) in the Joe the Bartender sketches.

Maybe because of the twelve kids he had to feed, Gleason felt sorry for Fontaine, and played straight for him. The usual routine was for the invisible Mr. Dennehey

□

in the barroom to ask if Crazy was around.

"Yeah," Joe would say, "he's out back."

Then Crazy would appear and start telling outrageous stories to Joe. All Gleason did was listen but the expressions on his face as he listened were masterpieces of reaction. Finally, Joe the bartender would ask Crazy to sing a song. Fontaine had a rich baritone voice and sang completely out of character. The audience ate it up.

During his successful run with Miami Beach television, Gleason did not neglect his blossoming movie career. In 1968, Gleason spent his summer hiatus doing a movie for Otto Preminger. When Preminger made hits like *Laura* and *The Man with the Golden Arm,* they were tremendous. But when he made flops, as he did with Gleason in *Skidoo,* they were really horrible. *Skidoo* did just that, in and out of the nation's theaters, at least those dumb enough to book it.

In the summer of 1968, Jackie also managed to fit in *How to Commit Marriage* with Bob Hope. Much of the picture was shot at Lakeside Golf Club near Hope's home in Toluca Lake, a suburb of Los Angeles. Gleason claims that he made more money off golf bets with Hope than he got for working in the movie.

"Gleason is a fraud on the golf course," says Hope. "Whenever I putted, Gleason's breath would melt my putter."

Nevertheless, one of Gleason's prize photos is of Hope paying off a five-hundred-dollar golf bet.

"Hope handing over so much money on the golf course makes that picture worth more than an original Picasso. It's a collector's item."

In 1968–69 and again in 1969–70, the Jackie Gleason show rolled merrily along, high in the ratings. It looked as if The Great One were indestructible on the tube. Then, in the spring of 1970, Bob Wood, who was then president of

CBS, discovered a new word that had been coined on Madison avenue—*demographics.*

It was an advertising term that meant that it didn't matter how many people watched your program, but only who they were. Advertisers, said Madison Avenue, wanted to reach the eighteen-to-thirty-four age group. In a pinch, they might go as high as forty-nine. If you were over fifty and going broke buying the sponsors' products, you didn't exist on Madison Avenue.

This posed a dilemma for Fred Silverman, chief of programming for CBS. Three of his highest-rated shows were attracting too old an audience. At the close of the 1970–71 season, Red Skelton got canceled after twenty-three years on weekly television, still the record for comedy. Worse, his show was in fifth place in the ratings. "Petticoat Junction," another top-rated show, was attracting too bucolic an audience. It got the ax too. And this from the same network that had made millions off "The Beverly Hillbillies."

Jackie, earning $205,000 a week, asked for a raise at the wrong time. He got the pink slip too, because he asked for too much money—and because of demographics.

And so, for Sheila MacRae as Alice Kramden and Meredith MacRae as a star of "Petticoat Junction," there was the dubious honor of being the only mother and daughter ever canceled at the same time.

· 15 ·
GLEASON
FREE

The year 1971 was a land-mark year for Jackie Gleason. He was no longer the king of Saturday night television. He got a divorce from wife Gen after thirty-five years of marriage, most of which had been in name only. And he got married to a girl none of his friends had ever heard of, almost on the very day he got his divorce.

Bob Wood, whose love of demographics canceled the Gleason show, recalls: "We were victims of our own success. We were just attracting more older people than young. Television was a whole new ball game on Madison Avenue. Sponsors wanted the younger crowd. We found our greatest strength in rural counties, instead of the big cities."

□

Gleason admits that his viewers had remained loyal to him from the Dumont days in 1950 through 1971. Only problem was that they were now twenty-one years older. "The network thought that my viewers weren't buying anything, yet they sure as hell had more money to spend than the young crowd just getting started with all the expenses of raising their families."

Ironically, in 1983 the Public Broadcasting System started a program called "The Best of Gleason," showing sketches from the 1962–71 "American Scene Magazine." KCET, the PBS station in Los Angeles, reports that the show attracted such a young audience that after nearly two years on an 11 P.M. time slot, the station moved the show to 6 P.M., in order to capture an even bigger youth following. So much for demographics.

Jackie, naturally, was hurt by CBS president Wood's rejection of his Saturday night show from Miami Beach in 1971, but he wasn't as bitter about the cancellation as Red Skelton. Red threatened to burn all twenty-three years of his tapes. He still says that CBS will never see any excerpts from his shows, which he owns.

When Gleason's show was canceled, it was always in the top fifteen shows and very often in the first ten. Wood recalls that "it was a very agonizing decision to make." A couple of other factors were involved in the decision, whether CBS admits it or not. Gleason's asking for a raise on his $205,000 a week salary must have helped. And there was also the debut of "All in the Family" in 1971. "All in the Family" was not a direct steal on "The Honeymooners." Ralph Kramden was not a bigot like Archie Bunker. But the shows were too similar to be on the same network in the same season. There was just no way Ralph Kramden and Archie Bunker could coexist.

□

It would be interesting to compare the demographics between the two shows. No one at CBS is willing to come up with those sacrosanct numbers.

In 1972, Gleason's fifteen-year, $100,000-a-year fringe benefit contract with CBS expired. He did not try to renew with the network that had dropped him. He signed instead with NBC, but that only lasted a year when that network couldn't come up with any suitable program for him.

About the only thing that came out of the NBC tenure was a Dean Martin roast, produced by Greg Garrison. It was a hilarious affair, and ABC immediately became interested in Gleason. Once again, though, a network couldn't come up with anything that would get Gleason back on weekly television.

Part of the problem was Gleason himself. A few days after he got his no-fault divorce decree from Gen in 1971, he had married Beverly McKittrick, a girl he had started dating at the Miami Beach Country Club after the departure of Honey Merrill.

"I married Beverly in England within days after the state of Florida enacted its no-fault divorce law. I felt I was free at last and I had to marry someone right away." (Some people might argue with that. Jackie had been a swinging bachelor much of his successful life.)

He divorced Beverly in 1974, after three years of mostly playing golf and drinking martinis.

"Beverly was a nice girl," says Jackie. "In fact, every girl I ever went with was nice. And every girl I ever married was nice."

Although he signed with ABC in 1973, Jackie seemed to prefer the golf course. The network offered him big money for a weekly return to television, but Gleason, sitting in his well-stocked golf cart, asked, with some logic,

"Look at that beautiful golf course. Look at that blue sky with a few puffy clouds. Why would anyone want to work with a life like this?"

Whether it was golf, diet, cosmetic surgery, or whatever, Gleason's weight dropped from its onetime high of 289 pounds in the CBS days to 205 pounds in the early and mid-seventies.

Real Estate developers approached him with the idea of lending his name to the famous Inverrary Country Club at Lauderhill, Florida, where he still lives. His name, still magic, helped sell homes on the golf course, which appealed to Jackie's sense of the grandiose.

"We have five championship courses, two more than any other course in the country."

For years, the Jackie Gleason Inverrary Classic was a regular stop on the PGA tour. His Celebrity Pro-Am attracted all his show-business friends, from Bob Hope to Bing Crosby.

(He abruptly took his name off the tournament as 1980 approached. "You know me, I'm first-cabin all the way. I just didn't like the way the sponsors were cutting corners on my friends.")

In return for all this, the developers of Inverrary gave Jackie a magnificent home on one of the fairways. This was in 1973, and the house then was worth a million. Completely rebuilt now, it's worth twice that.

The house was unlike the million-dollar round house, reminiscent of a flying saucer, that CBS had built for him in Peekskill, New York.

The Inverrary house was more traditional, something that old money like the Whitneys or Vanderbilts might live in at Palm Beach, a little farther up the coast. Instead of the twelve bars, it had one magnificent bar that would have

□

done justice to the old Toots Shor's saloon. In fact, it was reminiscent of Toots' circular bar, now torn down. Jackie himself designed the barstools, from which it was impossible to fall off.

"I would have defied any of my old drinking pals like Toots or Bogie, both dead now, to fall off those stools. Even W. C. Fields would have felt safe in them."

Naturally, the Gleason home in Inverrary had the usual status symbol—a poolroom. Willie Mosconi, the billiards champ, designed it. The pool table was in the only room in the house that Jackie didn't design. It was in a sunken arena and looked like the site of the world's pocket billiard championships.

Jackie and Beverly lived in the house for the first year, and when they divorced in 1974, Beverly tried to get the house in the property settlement. Jackie held on to it and gave her money instead. He was used to that, since he had given millions to Gen over the years. "It's the law," he says philosophically.

Jackie and Marilyn married quietly in 1975. None of Gleasons' friends in Hollywood knew about the wedding until Christmas of 1975; the Christmas cards that year were signed "Jackie and Marilyn Gleason."

On February 2, 1976, Jackie, Art, Audrey and Jane Kean reunited for the celebration on ABC of the twenty-fifth anniversary of "The Honeymooners," which also marked the twenty-fifth wedding anniversary of the Kramdens. It was the year of the nation's bicentennial, and it was fitting that there should be an anniversary for one of television's national treasures.

For Jackie, the show—before a live audience as always—was exciting. He sat in a chair before his opening cue like a racehorse in the starting gate. He said, "Art and

Audrey and Jane moved into this thing like they had all been doing it for weeks. They never were away."

The only difference in the show from former years was that it aired from Miami, instead of Miami Beach. The city of Miami got its money's worth: Jackie opened the show singing "Moon Over Miami," and mentioned the city fifteen times, even though he was supposedly in an old Brooklyn tenement.

The show got big ratings, and Gleason took off afterward for Palm Springs, where he was the guest of Bob Hope in one of three homes Hope owns in the California desert city.

It was a new Gleason who joined up with Hope and former President Gerald Ford in the Bob Hope Desert Classic. Gleason did jokes for eighteen holes on Hope's wealth, a subject Hope doesn't want to publicize.

At a party at Hope's house one night, everybody was drinking champagne or vodka, except Jackie. He was drinking Tab, the diet cola.

Hope called a photographer to hurry over. "I want a picture of Gleason with a soft drink. I want to hang it in my living room," said Hope.

Gleason is not as wealthy as Hope, but Jackie has a few bucks. For instance, on that same trip west, Jackie gave his old pal Jack Haley sixty thousand dollars to invest in a real estate deal. Flo Haley said that within a year, her Jack mailed Gleason a check for one million, a nice return on an investment.

"Haley was the shrewdest real estate investor I have ever known," says Jackie. "When he first started hitting it big in the movies back in the thirties, he bought eight blocks in Beverly hills for a song—both sides of Wilshire Boulevard in downtown Beverly Hills."

Jack Haley, Jr., who now runs his father's holdings, says: "I am still mailing checks back to Gleason all the time on investments my father made for him. Jackie put so much faith in my father's business judgment that he asked my father to be the executor of his estate in case Jackie should die first."

Jackie outlived his old pal.

Gleason claims he took back a wad of golf money won from Hope in Palm Springs. Hope denies this. "The only money he left with was what he got from Goodyear by hiring himself out as a standby blimp."

Back in Florida, it was a summer and fall of daily golf at Inverrary. And when 1976 passed into 1977, it was more golf. Jackie was getting used to the good life. That year (1977) Burt Reynolds asked him to play a redneck southern sheriff in *Smokey and the Bandit,* but it only caused a short disruption of Jackie's golf game.

Gleason still had a deal with ABC, and after the good ratings from the anniversary show, they wanted him back. While sitting in his barber chair one day, Jackie dreamed up an idea for a Christmas special.

Ralph is still a bus driver for the Gotham Bus company, but he and Alice are going to Miami for a winter vacation. His boss ruins that by saying he wants Ralph to direct Dickens' *A Christmas Carol* for his wife's charity, a home for stray cats. Alice and Ralph play the Cratchits, while Ed Norton is a hilarious Scrooge and Tiny Tim, sometimes getting the wigs mixed up. Alice and Trixie paint cornflakes white to look like snow, only the snow falls like a ton of bricks on the cast instead of trickling down.

The boss is so grateful, he presents Ralph with a pregnant cat—and promotes him to traffic manager, at last.

There were more big ratings, and ABC wanted a Valentine's Day special to follow a few months later, on February 13, 1978. In it, Ralph buys Alice an all-electric kitchen as a surprise Valentine's Day gift. It overloads the circuit in the tiny flat, and the first time he demonstrates it, it explodes in front of fifty million people. "The Honeymooners" thus went out with a big bang.

In 1978, George C. Scott revived *The Sly Fox* on Broadway, and Jackie, his old co-star from *The Hustler,* toured with the national company. Scott caught Jackie in the road company in San Diego and told a *San Diego Union* reporter: "Jackie does it better than I."

When the play reached Chicago in the fall of 1978, Jackie was nearing the end of the last act when he got severe chest pains onstage. He was having a heart attack, but he didn't realize it.

Mary Agnes Patton, a secretary, was in the audience that night. She says, "I thought that poor man was going to die onstage. He was fighting for his breath, gasping, but he kept on. I kept hoping they would ring down the curtain. But he finished the play."

Jackie himself recalls those horrible few moments. "I was pleading with my eyes for the other actors to speed up their lines so I could get offstage. It's the first time in my career where I almost walked offstage without finishing a show. Somehow, I got through it and when the curtain went down, the pains stopped as suddenly as they had started.

"I thought it must have been heartburn or something, so after the performance, I took Marilyn to an Italian restaurant for some spaghetti and vino. That did it. The pains came on again in the restaurant and next thing I was in an ambulance with the paramedics working over me.

"It didn't scare me. I thought sure this was the final curtain. Death, somehow, didn't frighten me."

Doctors immediately performed a heart bypass operation. Jackie himself doesn't remember whether it was a triple or quadruple. (It was a triple.) "Who's counting at a time like that?" When he woke up in intensive care later that day, he immediately asked for a cigarette.

"Marilyn gave me holy hell and told me I would never smoke again. I got out of bed and walked down the hall with all the nurses and doctors chasing me. I got my cigarette and some booze too. My wife, by this time, was really madder than hell at me, but I was going to smoke, come hell or high water.

"The next day, I wanted a shower. About four hundred doctors came out of the walls and said I couldn't have a shower; the showers were about a quarter mile down the hall.

"So I got out of bed and walked down the hall in my nightshirt and took a shower, bandages and all. Marilyn gave up on me and told the nurses to give me anything I wanted; I'd get it anyhow."

About the only good news that came out of 1978 were the box-office receipts from *Smokey and the Bandit,* the movie he had made the year before with Burt Reynolds. In general release, it had climbed to a $61 million gross, and it was rated number fourteen in the all-time list of box-office blockbusters.

"I knew when Burt and Hal Needham the director wanted me to play that sheriff, I had to come up with something different. The redneck sheriff had been done too often before. That's why I drew the pencil mustache and came up with the expression 'Sumbitch.' Like some of my television lingo, it became part of the national and international jargon. Unfortunately, too many kids picked up on that one."

(The movie even made Jackie something of a cult figure among Great Britain's youth. Proper Etonians were shocking their aristocratic parents by muttering "Sumbitch" at the dinner table.)

All of a sudden, Gleason had a movie renaissance—nothing will accomplish that more quickly than $61 million gross. When a picture makes that kind of money, even the grips who worked on it get more offers than they can handle.

On this score, Jackie is downright humble for a change: "I know I'm a good actor but I have no special attraction for people who go to see movies. I don't have a motion picture personality. I can make a guy who has one look better than he is. That's my appeal as an actor."

Jackie is downgrading himself a bit there. For *Smokey and the Bandit II,* made in 1980, Jackie got better than one million dollars. Producers don't shell out that kind of money unless there is a proven track record at the box office.

Hal Needham says, "The chemistry between Reynolds and Gleason is what made *Smokey* the huge success it was. Same with the second one. That grossed better than $38 million, real big for a sequel."

(*Smokey and the Bandit III,* only starring Gleason, made money, too—but it was nothing like its predecessors.)

Gleason's observation that he can make a movie personality look better than he is has some basis in fact. Reynolds, a king of the box office, has had some trouble there since the two *Smokey* movies. Of course, serious illness has played an important role in Burt's troubles with selling tickets. (In April 1985, *Boxoffice Magazine* knocked Burt from its list of the top four male stars, the first time that had happened in five years. During the *Smokey* movies he was either tied with Clint Eastwood or held the number-one spot outright.)

Gleason says he is looking for a property for Burt so that The Great One can make his directorial debut. "I don't believe Burt, especially as a comedic actor, has as yet realized a fraction of his potential. I think I can bring that out in him," says Jackie.

Chemistry between two actors doesn't always exist. In *The Sting II*, Jackie was paired with Mac Davis. The casting didn't come off when the two of them worked together, although in Jackie's scenes with Karl Malden, it did. That movie was made in 1981, and did well at the box office, but nothing sensational. Jackie says it was "a terrible movie," something you don't often hear an actor say about his own films.

"It gave me a chance to visit a lot with my daughters, who both live in Los Angeles," says Jackie.

(Jackie has two beautiful daughters, both black-haired and Irish-looking. Geraldine is married to a successful insurance executive, Jack Chutuk, who insured such diverse enterprises as the Pope's tour of the United States and the 1985 tour of Michael Jackson and his brothers. Daughter Linda, former wife of the Pulitzer Prize–winning playwright and actor Jason Miller [*That Championship Season*], is herself a successful actress. On Broadway, she was nominated for a Tony award for *Black Picture Show* in 1976. In 1983, she starred with Ralph Waite ["The Waltons"] in the television series *Mississippi*. Jackie has four grandchildren, none of them a comedian yet.)

In 1982, Jackie was teamed with Richard Pryor in *The*

Toy, a pairing that looked, on paper, to have been made in heaven. It didn't turn out that way.

The director had a new Laurel and Hardy to work with. Instead, he had Gleason play straight to Pryor and Pryor play straight to the brat kid in the movie. As it turned out, it was a comedy with no laughs, starring two of the funniest men on earth.

Gleason uses the same word—*terrible*—in giving his appraisal of that movie. (He also uses the same word to describe *Smokey and the Bandit III,* made the same year.)

The Toy, due to the teaming of Gleason and Pryor, was a huge box-office success, earning more than $55 million, despite disastrous critical notices. All the critics said the same thing: The movie was a complete waste of superior comedy talent.

After these two movies, Gleason was back in the hospital again for his second bypass in 1983. He came out of that one and asked his doctor if he had done a good job. The doctor told him he had. "Okay," said Jackie, "that means I'm as good as before." The doctor nodded agreement. So Jackie immediately started chain-smoking cigarettes, six packs a day. If he feels like it, he'll knock off six double Scotches at a sitting.

One day in 1983, in the Polo Lounge of the Beverly Hills Hotel, Jackie asked, "Jim, how do guys like you and me survive?"

"Because we're both Irish," I answered, "and the Irish are always trying to kill themselves but rarely succeed."

"Let's drink to that," said Jackie. "And also to Jack Oakie, the greatest comedy actor. For fifty years, Oakie drank a quart of Scotch a night. He lets his doctor talk him out of drinking and in six months, he's dead. That's as good a reason as any not to quit drinking."

Wife Marilyn is content with Jackie's life-style. She

knows she will never change him. "I used to have great concern but not anymore. Surprisingly, his lungs are as pure as a baby's. So is his heart. And how could I ever stop him from doing something that he enjoys so much?

"Our life down here in Florida is filled with sunshine, golf, love and contentment. We both have mellowed some."

What is life with Jackie like? Is he really Reggie Van Gleason?

"No," says Marilyn. "He's Ralph Kramden."

Jackie himself, when not playing golf, watches mostly sports on television. Sometimes he watches good dramas, like "Masterpiece Theatre," on PBS.

"As for comedians, everybody wants to do stand-up. Television cries for good sketch comedians, but there aren't any. The future is pay television, like HBO. The best thing I've done in years was *Mr. Halpern and Mr. Johnson* on HBO, with Laurence Olivier."

Many critics thought that Jackie more than held his own with the actor most people think is the world's greatest.

When Olivier was in Hollywood for the 1985 Oscars, he called Gleason one of the finest actors he had ever worked with.

"It was a wonderful experience for me. I was ill at the time and Jackie treated me like an angel of mercy. I had always admired him as a great comedian but now I admire him as a great serious actor. If I sound like a Jackie Gleason fan, it's because I am."

In February of 1985, Gleason unearthed seventy-five unseen "Honeymooners" from a vault where he had been paying a hundred bucks a week just to keep them at the proper temperature. These are the CBS shows, which were taped live from 1952–56. Why did Gleason wait so long to dig up this new batch of shows?

"I figured that thirty years was about as long as those filmed shows would run. They've been on longer than *Tobacco Road* and *Chorus Line*. I'll let these new ones run another thirty years and then I've got some more, the musical ones, with Sheila MacRae and Jane Kean. Those girls won't have to depend on social security."

Gleason says that the long-running success of "The Honeymooners" is due to its real-life situations.

Art Carney, for his part, is looking to collect more residuals. "I didn't have as good a lawyer as Audrey did. Mine ran out twenty-five years ago on the thirty-nine."

Art is living up in Westbrook, Connecticut, these days, with the Oscar he won in 1975 for *Harry and Tonto* on the mantel.

"I've got a nice house right on the beach in this small town. I've got six grandchildren. Two of my kids live here and another one lives in upstate New York. I read scripts and do what I want to do. It's a good life."

What does Art have to say about the success of "The Honeymooners"?

"As far as Jackie and I go, we had some kind of Irish chemistry working for us. I had never heard of him until I did that first Dumont show. He's been good to me, professionally and monetarily, over the years.

"We both have good senses of humor. We were never jealous of each other. Neither tried to upstage the other. Jackie always gave me all the freedom I wanted."

And how about that show that Jackie says was completely ad-libbed?

"I have to be honest with you, I don't ever remember a show that was completely ad-libbed. I know we did a lot of ad-libbing on shows in character and it always worked."

Perhaps the greatest example of this was in 1952, when

□

Gleason went into the bedroom and forgot to come back. Audrey followed him through the door, looking for him. The show was live and being seen by millions right then and Carney was left alone on the stage for two minutes. It was not part of the script.

Art went to the old icebox and did a few funny things, looking for something to eat. Finally, he found an orange. For the next ninety seconds, Art sat at the kitchen table and peeled an orange, with hilarious results. Gleason, who had gone looking for a Kleenex to mop his perspiring brow, finally came back through the door and did a double-take at Carney peeling an orange.

One other question of Art:

"Who is going to play Ralph and Ed Norton if they ever make 'The Honeymooners' into a Broadway musical, as was proposed for 1986?"

Replies Art: "I don't see how they can ever pull that off. I don't think it will happen."

The same question was asked of June Taylor.

"There's no way they can get actors to take the place of that quartet. The only way that show would ever work is to go completely in the opposite direction. Listen to this. Don't think me weird, but how about Danny DeVito playing Ralph and his wife, Rhea Perlman, who is on 'Cheers,' playing Alice? That's the only way you can go with that show. There never will be another Gleason or Carney or Audrey or Joyce or Jane."

I have an even better casting. Two of the most rabid fans of "The Honeymooners" are rock stars Bruce Springsteen and Cyndi Lauper. After all, Broadway musical comedy needs good singers, and both Cyndi and Bruce are members of RALPH, which makes them official Honeymoonies.

"I watch 'The Honeymooners' religiously. And

□

RALPH is the only fan club I have ever joined," says Cyndi. Springsteen feels the same way.

Will Gleason ever go back to weekly television?

"Never," he says.

But when you spend a lot of time with Gleason in movie dressing rooms, you get the idea that The Great One misses running the show as he did on television.

"All you do in the movies is get on the set at 9 A.M. and wait around all day for them to do your scene at 4 P.M., if you're lucky. Why in the hell can't they time movie production better? It was a lot more fun back in the old television days. A lot more fun."

One final note. With all his success and money, Jackie still has a trunk addressed to the Empire Burlesque Theater in Newark.

"I got a couple suits in there stuffed with ten-dollar bills. The guy who ran the Empire once told me if the bubble burst, I could always have my old job back as house comic. But is the Empire still there?

"Anyway you look at it, I have had a wonderful life. Considering the way it started out, I'm lucky to be alive.

"Look what happened to us in 1983. I'm in the hospital for an operation and Marilyn takes a room there to be near me. Our house at Inverrary catches fire from a faulty air conditioner and burns in minutes to the ground.

"Thank heavens, neither of us was in the place. We could both be part of a sand trap on the Inverrary golf course today."

☐

▪ APPENDIX ▪

FILMS

NOTE: Dates given are for year of release, which may vary from date of production.

Navy Blues. 1941. Directed by Lloyd Bacon. Starred three people who became lifelong friends of Gleason's—Jack Haley, Jack Oakie, and Martha Raye. Another Jack in the movie was the late Jack Carson.

All Through the Night. 1942. Directed by Vincent Sherman. This had about as potent a cast as Warners could muster in those early days of World War II. It starred Humphrey Bogart, Conrad Veidt, Jane Darwell, Frank McHugh, Peter Lorre, Judith Anderson, and William Demarest, and paired two burlesque comics who later would hit it big in television—Phil Silvers and Gleason.

□

Tramp Tramp Tramp. 1942. Directed by Charles Barton. Starred Florence Rice (the daughter of the famed sportswriter, Grantland Rice), Bruce Bennett, and Jack Durant. Gleason and Durant played a couple of 4-F civilians who thwart a murder.

Larceny Inc. 1942. Directed by Lloyd Bacon. This was the funniest of all Gleason's early movies but he only played a bit part as a soda jerk. The stars were Edward G. Robinson, Jane Wyman (then married to an actor who later went into politics, Broderick Crawford), Jack Carson, Anthony Quinn, and Edward Brophy. Brophy, Robinson, and Crawford play ex-convicts who use a luggage store as a front for nefarious activities. One of those classic little comedies that Robinson often made in those days when he wasn't playing "Little Caesar."

Springtime in the Rockies. 1942. Directed by Irving Cummings. Warners loaned out Jackie to 20th Century–Fox to play Betty Grable's manager in a musical that helped make her World War II's favorite pin-up. Harry James' band, with Helen Forrest singing, introduced the standard "I Had the Craziest Dream." Other stars were John Payne, Carmen Miranda, Cesar Romero, Charlotte Greenwood, and Edward Everett Horton. Gleason says he got a doctorate in scene-stealing by watching Horton work.

Orchestra Wives. 1942. Directed by Archie Mayo. Still on loanout to Fox, Jackie played a bass fiddle player in Glenn Miller's orchestra. Starred George Montgomery, Lynn Bari, Carole Landis, Cesar Romero, Ann Rutherford, Virginia Gilmore, and Mary Beth Hughes. Turned out to be the most profitable of all Gleason films because he formed a lasting friendship with trumpet virtuoso Bobby Hackett, then with Miller's band. Hackett would later be the soloist on Gleason's romantic albums, which sold in the millions. This picture marked the end of Gleason's contract at Warner Bros.

The Desert Hawk. 1950. Directed by Frederick De Cordova. Jackie reactivated his movie career by playing a blue-eyed Arab in this one. Another actor with a small part in the movie was Rock Hudson. Freddie De Cordova is now producer of "The Tonight Show" on NBC-TV. Other stars were Richard Greene, Yvonne De Carlo, and George Macready. This is the last film Jackie made in the fifties, since television stardom was just around the corner.

The Hustler. 1961. Directed by Robert Rossen. Jackie gave a memorable performance as Minnesota Fats. His Brooklyn pool hustling paid off in an Oscar-nominated performance. Jackie should have won an Oscar that year, but it was the year of *The West Side Story* sweep and dancer George Chakiris went home with the gold statuette for Best Supporting Actor. Paul Newman, Piper Laurie, George C. Scott, and Myron McCormick made up the rest of the great cast.

Gigot. 1962. Directed by Gene Kelly. This movie, shot in Paris, was a tour de force for Gleason. He ranks it as his favorite movie and he gave a superb performance in it. It's the story of a sad-faced deaf mute and a little girl. Chaplinesque in its style and acting.

Requiem for a Heavyweight. 1962. Directed by Ralph Nelson. This picture marked the film debut of Muhammad Ali (then known as Cassius Clay), who played one of the fighters. The stars, besides Jackie, were Tony Quinn,

Mickey Rooney, Julie Harris, Nancy Cushman, and Madame Spivy in a script written by Rod Serling from his original television drama. Jackie played the manager of an over-the-hill fighter (Quinn) and once more established himself as a serious dramatic actor.

Soldier in the Rain. 1963. Directed by Ralph Nelson. Starring Jackie, Steve McQueen, Tuesday Weld, Tony Bill, and Tom Poston. Blake Edwards wrote the script. Gleason was in his element as a swinging sergeant.

Papa's Delicate Condition. 1963. Directed by George Marshall. This was another tour de force for Jackie, who played the tipsy railroad inspector who was the real life father of silent star Corinne Griffith. Great cast—Glynis Johns, Charlie Ruggles, Charlie Lane, Laurel Goodwin, Elisha Cook, Jr., Juanita Moore, and Murray Hamilton. "Call Me Irresponsible" was the Oscar-winning song from the picture. George Marshall, one of Hollywood's all-time great comedy directors, always said that Gleason's performance in this movie should have rated another crack at the Oscar: "He would have won it if the Academy had nominated him as they should have." (This picture finished shooting in the summer of 1962 and once more television drew Jackie away from Hollywood and a good movie career.)

Skidoo. 1968. Directed by Otto Preminger. The only thing historic about this picture is that it was Groucho Marx's last. He played a mob godfather. Can you imagine a movie with Gleason and Groucho that would flop? It had an all-star cast in Carol Channing, Frankie Avalon, Fred Clark, Michael Constantine, Frank Gorshin, John Philip Law, Peter Lawford, Burgess Meredith, George Raft, Cesar Romero, Mickey Rooney, and Austin Pendleton.

□

Don't Drink the Water. 1969. Directed by Howard Morris. From the Woody Allen play about a family held captive in a fictional Iron Curtain country called Vulgaria. It didn't come off as well as Woody's Broadway show, despite a good comedy cast with Gleason, Estelle Parsons, Ted Bessell, Joan Delaney, Michael Constantine, Howard St. John, and Avery Schreiber.

How to Commit Marriage. 1969. Directed by Norman Panama. This was a movie that was hilarious to watch being made but didn't come off as great comedy on screen, despite the co-starring of Bob Hope and Gleason. Much of it was shot at Lakeside Golf Club near Hope's home in Toluca Lake, California, and the off-the-camera repartee was hilarious. Hope said Gleason owned the only golf cart with a bartender on it. "He putts with swizzle sticks." Gleason countered with jokes about Hope's money. "He still has those big dollar bills." They should have filmed the ad lib jokes and dumped the movie. Another good cast. Jane Wyman, Maureen Arthur, Leslie Neilsen, Tina Louise, and Professor Irwin Corey, who also was funnier off camera.

Smokey and the Bandit, I, II, III. 1977, 1980, 1983. First two directed by Hal Needham. Gleason wishes he had also directed the third. The first was a smash and gave movie audiences the potent box-office teaming of Gleason and Burt Reynolds. Not since Art Carney had Gleason found the magic comedy chemistry he and Burt had. Burt was only in the first two. The second *Smokey* had the same cast—Sally Field, Paul Williams, Pat McCormick, Jerry Reed, and Mike Henry. In 1983, producers had the idea that Gleason should play both Smokey and the Bandit without Burt. On the first day of shooting, Jackie said it wouldn't work. *Smokey and the Bandit III* had to be reshot with Jerry Reed playing the bandit, and even that didn't save it. Colleen Camp, McCormick, Williams, and Henry were in the third *Smokey*.

The Toy. 1982. Directed by Richard Donner. Once again the tremendous box-office appeal of Gleason and Richard Pryor was manifest in a movie that missed. It should have been a classic, with two of the hottest comedians in the business, but Donner, for the most part, kept them separated. It was the number one Christmas hit of 1982, racking up a quick $55 million gross. Pryor played a modern-day slave in the Deep South—that may have been the reason for his mysterious twelve-day disappearance from the set in the middle of shooting. Had that racist theme been directed for black comedy, it might have worked. Blame this one on the director and writer, not the stars who worked valiantly to save it. Also starred Ned Beatty, Wilfrid Hyde-White, and Teresa Ganzel.

Sting II. 1983. Directed by Jeremy Paul Kagan. Didn't come off like the original with Robert Redford and Paul Newman because comedy casting was lacking between Gleason and Mac Davis. Had Karl Malden and Davis switched roles, it would have worked, because Gleason and Malden worked like Laurel and Hardy together. The cast featured Oliver Reed and Teri Garr (daughter of the old-time comedian-actor, Eddie Garr.) It was a man's picture, but sexy Teri seemed to come off best.

Major Television Shows

Note: This does not include the many guest shots with Bob Hope, Lucille Ball, et cetera, nor appearances on such news shows as "Good Morning, America," "The Today Show," "CBS Morning News" and the like, all of which would make the list too cumbersome.

"Toast of the Town" (later to become "The Ed Sullivan Show"). In 1948, Jackie made his television debut on Ed's show. (Sullivan, a top Broadway columnist with the New York *Daily News,* was a habitué of the famous Club 18 and a fan of Jackie's insult humor.) Jackie did a sketch of a frustrated pinball player and was such a hit that Sullivan wanted him back immediately. He couldn't make it because an important radio writer in Hollywood saw a kinescope of Jackie on the Sullivan show—Jackie's next stop was Hollywood.

"The Life of Riley." From October 1949 to March 1950, Jackie played Chester A. Riley, a riveter at Stephenson Aircraft in Los Angeles. It had been one of radio's most popular radio shows, starring the late William Bendix, from 1944 to 1949. Bendix, under contract to RKO Pictures, couldn't do television in those days, when movie studios thought the infant medium an upstart. (Movie studios today would be parking lots and shopping centers if the movies and television hadn't joined forces in the fifties.) Twenty-six episodes were filmed for NBC-TV; this was one of television's first situation comedies. Like the later "The Honeymooners," it was a forerunner of Archie Bunker and "All in the Family." Rosemary DeCamp played Jackie's wife, Gloria Winters his daughter, Lanny Rees his son, Junior, and Sid Tomack his next-door neighbor. A riotous

□
203

character on the show was John Brown as the friendly neighborhood undertaker Digger O'Dell. There's no doubt that Digger Phelps, the Notre Dame basketball coach, got his nickname from this show—Phelps came from a family of morticians. This show gave Jackie national exposure, and he no longer was just a night club comic known only by the Hollywood and Broadway crowd. It was writer-producer Irving Brecher who saw that Ed Sullivan kinescope and knew he had found his television Riley.

"Dumont Cavalcade of Stars." 1950–52. This is the show that made Jackie Gleason a star. It was here that the nation first saw Reggie Van Gleason the Third, The Poor Soul, Joe the Bartender, and the seemingly immortal Ralph Kramden. With Pert Kelton as Alice and Art Carney as Ed Norton, "The Honeymooners" was first shown here.

"The Frank Sinatra Show." CBS. 1951–52. Gleason, at the urging of his old pal from the New Jersey days, did a half dozen guest shots on this show while still doing his "Dumont Cavalcade of Stars." Undoubtedly, this was the most important financial move Jackie ever made, although he refused to accept any fee from Frank. Bill Paley, founder of CBS, saw Gleason on the Sinatra show and immediately sent out word to his number-two man, Hubbell Robinson: "Get Gleason." In the fall of 1952, Jackie signed an eleven-million-dollar contract with CBS, then the highest in television history.

"The Jackie Gleason Show." CBS. From 1952 until this show's cancellation in 1971, Jackie Gleason dominated CBS-TV. He became a giant of television comedy in more ways than one; sometimes his weight ballooned to two-hundred-eighty pounds. With only slight periods off the air, he was Mr. Saturday Night on network television. In the early CBS years the show would start with a production number by the June Taylor dancers, who vied with the Rockettes as precision dancers, then follow with a bevy of beautiful GleaGirls in closeup introducing The Great One, who bounced in for his opening monologue. The monologue featured the famous Gleason expressions—"How sweet it is!" "A little traveling music, please," "Awa-a-a-y we go," and "Mmm. You're a good group." Following Gleason's monologue, there came the sketches—Reggie, Joe, The Poor Soul, Charley the Loudmouth, Pedro the Mexican, Stanley R. Sogg (the TV movie pitchman who always introduced a movie starring "the ever-popular Mae Busch"), Rum Dum, and many others. The second half of the show was "The Honeymooners," starring one of the all-time great comedy casts with Audrey Meadows as Alice, Art Carney as Ed Norton the sewer worker, and Joyce Randolph as his ex-stripper wife. Thirty-nine of these episodes were filmed in 1955, and they have been running ever since. On Thanksgiving Day, 1984, Channel 13 in Los Angeles ran all thirty-nine of them—from six A.M. until two A.M. the following morning, with ultra-high ratings. One New York station, WPIX, ran them every night for twenty-five years. The Gleason show, which started in New York, moved to Miami Beach in 1966, where "The Honeymooners" left their Brooklyn slum and sang and danced their way around the world with a new Alice (Sheila MacRae) and a new Trixie (Jane Kean). Since 1971, except for a few "Honeymooners" specials, Gleason has been mostly a movie star.

"Studio One." 1953. "The Laugh Maker." Jackie's serious dramatic debut in this prestigious drama series.

"The Golden Age of Jazz." 1959. This marked the emergence of the musical Jackie Gleason as opposed to the comedic or dramatic Gleason. He hosted this CBS show, which featured such legends as Louis Armstrong, Duke Ellington, Dizzy Gillespie, and George Shearing. This, too, like "Studio One," was a different side of the versatile comedian.

"You're in the Picture." In 1961, Gleason, on a hiatus from his regular show, performed in this show at the urging of some CBS bigshots. It was a prime-time game show in which celebrities stuck their heads into a huge photograph, then tried to guess what picture they were in. It was probably one of the worst shows in television history, closing after one show at Gleason's request. The next week, he apologized for the first show. For the remaining weeks of the contract, the show was renamed "The Jackie Gleason Show," and was a typical talk show.

THEATER

Keep Off the Grass. 1940. Jackie's legitimate theater debut. This show tried out for four weeks in Boston but lasted only three weeks in New York, despite a star-studded cast—Jimmy Durante, Jane Froman, Ray Bolger, and Virginia O'Brien. Louis B. Mayer of MGM saw Virginia in it and signed her to an MGM contract, after which she scored as a deadpan singer in a series of MGM musicals of the forties.

Hellzapoppin'. 1943. The national company, with Jackie and Lew Parker taking the Olsen and Johnson roles from the Broadway hit. If anything, Parker was as much a swinger as Gleason. He was also a great lover of horseflesh and womanflesh. If you thought the Broadway show was crazy, you should have seen these two in the touring company. It was lunacy every night at 8:30 P.M., and two matinees on Wednesday and Saturday.

Along Fifth Avenue. 1944. Everybody who has ever seen this musical comedy remembers only Jackie Gleason, including myself, who saw it while stationed temporarily in New York City as a naval officer at Third Naval District headquarters. This was the show wherein Gleason invented Reggie Van Gleason the Third in a French Foreign Legion sketch that had audiences laughing for five minutes solid. The show didn't quite make it, but Jackie did.

Follow the Girls. 1945–46. Jackie's co-star was the late and great Gertrude Neisen, who was one of the reigning queens of Broadway musical comedy of that era. Jackie's ad-lib humor made him tough to work with, but the laughs were so fast and plentiful, Gertrude soon learned to live with him—and joined in the fun, too. A hit show in every sense of the word, and another personal hit for Jackie.

Take Me Along. 1959. Jackie, who never won an Emmy in television, went off the medium to star as the drinking uncle in the musical comedy version of Eugene O'Neill's *Ah! Wilderness,* a warm nostalgic look at small-town life at the turn of the century. Jackie's role was relatively small but it won him the theater's prestigious Tony. Walter Pidgeon, Ruth Warrick, and Una Merkel co-starred with Jackie. Jackie and producer David Merrick had a running feud during the run, which only served to sell more tickets. A smash show.

The Sly Fox. 1978. National company. Jackie scored a personal triumph in this classic play, but it almost rang down the final curtain. In Chicago, he suffered a heart attack onstage in the final act but, with a trouper's instinct, finished the play. He then underwent a triple bypass operation.

▪ INDEX ▪

□

■ ABOUT THE AUTHOR ■

James Bacon is the last of the celebrity Hollywood columnists, having outlived his one-time contemporaries Louella Parsons and Hedda Hopper. Bacon, a working newspaperman since 1936, claims he was once legitimate, covering presidents of the United States from FDR to JFK, crowned heads of Europe, plane crashes, train wrecks, floods, brush fires and earthquakes like any good reporter.

Then in 1948, the Associated Press sent him out to Hollywood, where he has reported the pecadilloes and idiosyncracies of stars from Erroll Flynn, Bogie, Gable and Monroe, down to the current crop—from Eastwood to Michael Jackson. He's been everywhere and knows everybody. In 1968, when Louella retired, he left AP and moved to the *Los Angeles Herald Examiner*.

He is the author of two previous bestselling memoirs, *Made in Hollywood* and *Hollywood is a Four-Letter Town*.